THE ALLURE OF THE
AUTOMOBILE

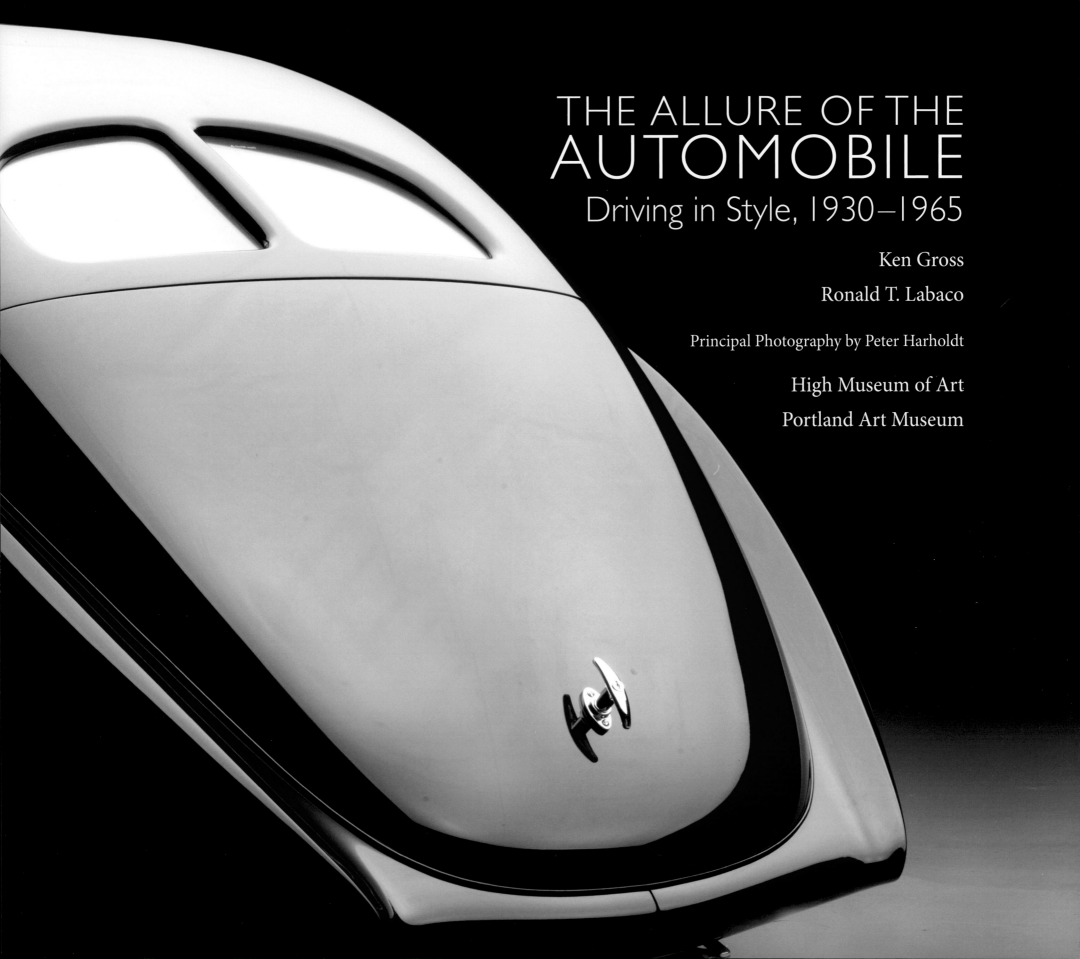

THE ALLURE OF THE
AUTOMOBILE
Driving in Style, 1930–1965

Ken Gross

Ronald T. Labaco

Principal Photography by Peter Harholdt

High Museum of Art

Portland Art Museum

The Allure of the Automobile is organized by the High Museum of Art, Atlanta, Georgia. The exhibition is made possible by

Lead Corporate Sponsor

Additional support provided by

Alfred and Adele Davis Exhibition Endowment
Eleanor McDonald Storza Exhibition Endowment
Howell Exhibition Endowment Fund
The Allure of the Automobile Society

Project Partner

ATLANTA
MIDTOWN

Major sponsors to the Portland Art Museum exhibition are

With additional support provided by

Wells Fargo
Bonhams & Butterfields
The Allure Society of the Portland Art Museum

Published on the occasion of the exhibition
The Allure of the Automobile: Driving in Style, 1930–1965

High Museum of Art, Atlanta   Portland Art Museum
March 21–June 20, 2010   Portland, Oregon
                                   June 11–September 11, 2011

Published by the High Museum of Art, in association with Skira Rizzoli

Second printing, 2011

Library of Congress Cataloging-in-Publication Data
Gross, Ken, 1941–
     The allure of the automobile: driving in style, 1930–1965 / essay by Ronald T. Labaco ; entries by Ken Gross.
       p. cm.
     Published on the occasion of an exhibition held at the High Museum of Art, Atlanta, Mar. 21–June 20, 2010.
     Includes index.
     ISBN 978-0-8478-3495-2 (alk. paper)
     1. Automobiles—
     Bodies. I. Labaco, Ronald T. II. High Museum of Art. III. Title.
     TL255.G75 2010
     629.222074>758231—dc22   2009051854

Details:
Front cover: See page 50
Page 1: See page 38
Pages 2–3: See page 74
Page 5: See page 80
Page 8: See page 86
Page 25: See page 68

Edited by Kelly Morris and Rachel Bohan
Designed by Angela J. Jaeger, assisted by Jeremy Linden
Coordinated by Berry Lowden
Proofread by Marie Weiler
Color management by iocolor, Seattle
Produced by Marquand Books, Inc., Seattle
Printed and bound by Shenzhen Artron Color Printing Co., Ltd., China

Contents

High Museum of Art
Acknowledgments

The idea of an exhibition to celebrate the beauty of classic automotive design came from Michael E. Shapiro, the High's Nancy and Holcombe T. Green, Jr. Director. I would like to extend my gratitude to him and David Brenneman, Director of Collections and Exhibitions, for their unflagging support. I extend my heartfelt appreciation to Ken Gross, guest curator of the exhibition.

I would like to thank the automobile lenders: Don Williams, Rob Williams, and the Blackhawk Collection (1933 Pierce-Arrow Silver Arrow); Bob and Sandra Bahre, and Jeff Orwig of the Robert Bahre Collection (1934 Packard LeBaron Runabout Speedster); Sam and Emily Mann (1935 Duesenberg JN Roadster and 1937 Delage D8-120S); William E. (Chip) Connor, Amy Canadas, and Susan Koesling (1937 Bugatti Type 57S Atalante); Merle and Peter Mullin, the Peter Mullin Automotive Museum Foundation, and Susan Bendrick (1937 Hispano-Suiza H-6C "Xenia"); Lee and Joan Herrington (1937 Mercedes-Benz 540K Special Roadster); Jon and Mary Shirley (1938 Alfa Romeo 8C2900B Touring Berlinetta); The Porsche Museum and Detlev von Platen, Bernd Harling, and Angie Reevers of Porsche Cars North America (1938–1939 Porsche Type 64); Mrs. Gene "Neta" Cofer and Charles R. "Chip" Cofer of the Cofer Collection, and Cecil D. McCall, Jr., curator of the Cofer Collection (1948 Tucker Model 48 Torpedo); Miles Collier and the Collier Collection, Scott George, Mark Patrick, and Jennifer Tobin (1953 Porsche 550); David J. Disiere and Tamara Wagner (1954 Dodge Firearrow III); Mercedes-Benz Museum Stuttgart, Dr. Josef Ernst, Geoff Day, Robert Moran, Adam Paige, and Matthew Butler (1955 Mercedes-Benz 300SLR "Uhlenhaut" Coupe); Gene and Marlene Epstein (1957 Cadillac Eldorado Brougham); Margie Petersen and the Petersen Automotive Museum, Dick Messer, Leslie Kendall, Tom Kenney, Chris Brown, and Mary Brisson (1957 Jaguar XK-SS Roadster); General Motors Heritage Center, Ed Welburn, Rodney Green, David Tellefsen, Larry Kinsel, and John Neuville (1959 Chevrolet Corvette Sting Ray); David Sydorick (1961 Aston Martin DB4GT Zagato); and Bruce Meyer (1961 Ferrari 250 GT Comp./61 Short-wheelbase Berlinetta).

I am thankful to my curatorial assistant at the High, Berry Lowden, for her research; to Philip Verre, Chief Operating Officer, for supporting the project; to Kelly Morris and Rachel Bohan for editing and managing the book; to Angela Jaeger for the design; and to Peter Harholdt for his photography.

I am grateful to Jack and Helen Nethercutt, Skip Marketti, and Lisa Delao of the Nethercutt Collection; Kandace Hawkinson and the Pebble Beach Concours d'Elegance; Ronald Kellogg; Ronald Benach; Richard Adatto; Michael Furman; Dennita Sewell, Leesha Allston, and Rebecca Dankert at the Phoenix Art Museum; Darcy Kuronen and Jennifer Riley at the Museum of Fine Arts, Boston; Jennifer Russell, Aidan O'Connor, Robert Kastler, Roberto Rivera, and The Museum of Modern Art, New York; Marie-Claude Saia at the Montréal Museum of Fine Arts; Ian Kelleher, Amy Christie, and Terry Lobzun at RM Auctions; Yann Saunders and Paul Ayres with the Cadillac and LaSalle Club; Jean-Michel Roux; Mark Steigerwald and the International Motor Racing Research Center at Watkins Glen; Danielle Szostak-Viers and the Chrysler Historical Collection; Faye McLeod and the Aston Martin Heritage Trust; Shana Hinds at Merciless Editing; Richard Lentinello and Daniel Strohl at Hemmings Motor News; Dwayne Cox, Joyce Hicks, and Linda Thornton at the Auburn University Libraries; Richard Day and the Bugatti Trust; Susan Accorto at Herrington Catalog; Michael Lamm and Lamm-Morada Publishing Co. Inc.; Virginia Graham at Creative Concepts Ink; Neil Rashba Photography; Tom Cotter; Ron Kimball, Debbie Callaway, and Melissa Allison at kimballstock; Charles Bronson; Jon Bill and the Auburn Cord Duesenberg Automobile Museum; Erin Chase, Manuel Flores, and The Huntington Library; Terry Bird; Murray Vise; Stephen Griswold; Ralph Marano; Arturo Keller; John Hendricks; Mike Tillson at Mike Tillson Motorcars; and Cristina Cheever at Starring You Marketing and Promotions. Special thanks go out to Webb Farrer at Webb Farrer Automotive Management Company Inc. for his expertise and guidance in handling these automotive masterworks.

Ronald T. Labaco

Portland Art Museum
Acknowledgments

Placing great objects in the context of an art museum creates a magical moment, allowing visitors to relish the object's beauty and importance. However, when those objects are automobiles—ubiquitous things that often overwhelm our lives—the visitor becomes intrigued and sometimes confused, questioning their presence in the museum. *The Allure of the Automobile* dispels these queries while simultaneously deepening our appreciation by presenting some of the finest crafted and most exquisitely designed objects in the world.

The presentation of a reconstituted *The Allure of the Automobile* at the Portland Art Museum, which features four new automobiles, owes much to the High Museum's director Michael Shapiro, and Director of Collections and Exhibitions David Brenneman. I am grateful to Michael and David for their willingness to travel the exhibition. Exhibition curator Ken Gross has been invaluable in reconceiving the exhibition. His deep knowledge and passion for automobile design and history have created once again a memorable exhibition. Photographer Peter Harholdt captured the artistry of the automobiles with exceptional images of the Portland additions.

Bob Ames, a past trustee of the Museum, automobile aficionado, and community leader, provided valuable counsel throughout the entire planning of the Portland version. I am indebted to Bob and his wife Kathleen for their many contributions as well as for chairing the Allure Society. Keith Martin, an authority on classic automobiles, has tirelessly advocated for the project. The Museum's Director of Operations Rob Bearden did an extraordinary job in positioning the exhibition within our community. My assistant Elizabeth Thomas, a valued partner on many tasks, provided meticulous administrative support and energy. Director of Development J. S. May and his team implemented a number of creative strategies to secure the necessary resources and attention. Additionally, Chief Curator Bruce Guenther gave excellent guidance on many aspects of the project, and Director of Collections Management Don Urquhart and Chief Preparator Matthew Juniper safely transported the automobiles to Portland and beautifully placed them within our galleries.

In addition to the Atlanta lenders who have agreed to lend to Portland, I would like to thank Tom Armstrong (1931 Duesenberg SJ 488 Durham Convertible Sedan), Arturo Keller (1937 T150SS Teardrop Talbot), Jolene and Bruce McCaw (1930 Bentley Gurney Nutting Coupe), and The LeMay Family Collection, compliments of LeMay—America's Car Museum (1948 Tucker Model 48 Torpedo) for sharing their priceless automobiles.

I am extremely grateful to the major supporters of the exhibition in Portland, including The Standard and their President and CEO Greg Ness, Vice President, External Affairs Justin Delaney, and Director of Public Affairs Bob Speltz; Key Bank and their District President and Museum trustee Brian Rice; and Chubb Group of Insurance Companies and their U.S. Marketing Manager Jim Fiske, Vice President Jill Abere and Senior Underwriting Officer Brandon Stewart. Their contributions are most appreciated.

Finally, I would like to recognize my father, Peter Ferriso, for instilling in me an appreciation for beautifully engineered machines, and my wife Amy and father-in-law, Jonathan Pellegrin, for indulging my fascination with automobiles.

Brian J. Ferriso
The Marilyn H. and Dr. Robert B. Pamplin Jr. Director
Portland Art Museum

Director's Foreword

The Allure of the Automobile examines the golden age of automotive design by celebrating some of the world's finest cars from the 1930s to the early 1960s. During this era of brilliantly designed automobiles, engineering combined with artistry and craftsmanship to produce objects of unparalleled beauty. Created for the privileged few, these luxurious, custom-built automobiles embodied speed, style, and elegance, exerting influence on art, fashion, and design. We hope the subject matter of this exhibition will serve the Museum's mission by expanding the experience of our traditional audience while also reaching out to new groups.

The idea for a car exhibition was inspired by a visit to Paris in association with the High Museum's *Louvre Atlanta* project. A small display of classic American sports cars at the entrance to my hotel captured my attention. I was fascinated by the beauty of the body design, the attention to fine detail, and the degree of talent needed to execute such work. The exhibition's concept was further developed and realized by our guest curator Ken Gross, an automotive industry authority and former director of the Petersen Automotive Museum in Los Angeles. I am also grateful to Ronald T. Labaco, the High's former curator of decorative arts and design, who provided creative and logistical support throughout this project.

We are indebted to the lenders, public and private, who agreed to part with their treasures. Generous support from Lead Corporate Sponsor Porsche Cars North America, with additional assistance from AkzoNobel, AutoTrader Classics, Manheim, NAPA, the Alfred and Adele Davis Exhibition Endowment, the Eleanor McDonald Storza Exhibition Endowment, the Howell Exhibition Endowment Fund, the Walter Clay Hill Family Foundation, The Allure of the Automobile Society, and W Atlanta Midtown, made the this exhibition possible in Atlanta. We are delighted that *The Allure of the Automobile* is having a rebirth in Portland with most of the same cars, supplemented by additional West Coast lenders and sponsored by The Standard, Key Bank, and Chubb Group of Insurance Companies.

Michael E. Shapiro
Nancy and Holcombe T. Green, Jr. Director
High Museum of Art

The Art of the Automobile:
The Supreme Creation of an Era

RONALD T. LABACO

I think that cars today are almost the exact equivalent of the great Gothic cathedrals: I mean the supreme creation of an era, conceived with passion by unknown artists, and consumed in image if not in usage by a whole population which appropriates them as a purely magical object.

Roland Barthes

The automobile is an emblem of modern society. It has sparked the imagination of artists, served as a vehicle for expression by designers and owners, and bolstered the economic growth of nations. In its nascence the automobile was embraced by the Futurist art movement as an iconoclastic symbol of industry, progress, and velocity. "We affirm that the world's magnificence has been enriched by a new beauty: the beauty of speed," wrote the Italian poet Filippo Tommaso Marinetti in his *Futurist Manifesto* of 1909. "A racing car whose hood is adorned with great pipes, like serpents of explosive breath . . . a roaring car that seems to ride on grapeshot is more beautiful than the Victory of Samothrace."

Almost half a century later, in 1951, The Museum of Modern Art in New York presented *Eight Automobiles*, an exhibition that put the design of the motor vehicle on par with modern art and architecture (fig. 1). "Automobiles are hollow, rolling sculpture," stated Arthur Drexler, the museum's curator of architecture and organizer of the show. "They have interior spaces corresponding to an outer form, like buildings, but the designer's aesthetic purpose is to enclose the functioning parts of an automobile, as well as its passengers, in a package suggesting directed movement along the ground."[1] Although unibody or unitary construction—in which the entire car, both body and machinery, were designed together—was growing in prevalence, Drexler made a clear distinction between the "functioning parts," or chassis, and the design of the "package," or body.

While the exhibition of automobiles was a first for a fine art museum, it was not out of character for MoMA, which has been a champion of modern design over the years. The institution's first design exhibition in 1934, *Machine Art*, asked the public to consider the aesthetic beauty of functional objects associated with industrial mass-production—including springs, propellers, and ball bearings—for their sculptural form, hard-edged geometric purity, and absolute utility.

The primary criterion for the selection of the works on display in both exhibitions was aesthetic. However, in contrast to the low-cost, utilitarian, proto-minimalist *Machine Art* objects, the *Eight Automobiles* exhibition included opulent, custom-designed, coachbuilt automobiles by such luxury manufacturers as Bentley, Mercedes-Benz, and Talbot-Lago, as well as several extremely well-designed production cars like the trendsetting 1949 Cisitalia by Pinin Farina and the 1937 Cord 812 designed by Gordon Buehrig. "Even though the American system of mass production does not encourage aesthetic speculation," wrote Drexler, "these cars contradict the claim that the American public prefers what is ugly, gross or even vulgar."[2] In these automobiles sculptural form and advanced mechanical engineering had combined to create rolling works of art.

During the golden age of the automobile, from the mid-1930s to the early 1960s, the beauty of car body design rested in the hands of the coachbuilder. Early motor cars comprised a rolling chassis—the engine, frame, suspension system, wheels, and steering mechanism supplied by an automotive manufacturer—and the body and passenger compartment, often designed and built by a coachbuilder. As a business, coachbuilding dated back to the introduction of the horse-drawn carriage. Rooted in the construction of coaches for the aristocracy, the "carriage trade" was a respectable and lucrative vocation, often a family enterprise passed down from one generation to the next; such was the case with several of the famous classic automotive coach-builders. And the products of the most talented workshops were equivalent to high-quality sculpture and the finest decorative arts.

Fig. 1. Installation view of the exhibition *Eight Automobiles*, The Museum of Modern Art, New York, August 28–November 11, 1951.

Early motorcar bodies were so similar to their horse-drawn precursors that they were often called "horseless carriages." Their form would remain relatively unchanged until Henry Ford revolutionized the industry with his dream of providing affordable and reliable transportation for the masses. "Design," he stated, "will take more advantage of the power of the machine to go beyond what the hand can do and will give us a whole new art."[3] Mechanization and mass-production were the determinant factors in the boxlike bodywork of the commercially successful Model T (fig. 2). In production from 1908 to 1927, the Ford Model T and its successor, the Model A (1928–1931), numbered in the millions. It was the ubiquity of these simple, straightforward motorcars across the United States and throughout western Europe that helped to usher in the era of the stylish automotive coachbuilder. Keen to affirm their privileged lifestyle, the social elite sought more opulent automobiles to distinguish their vehicles from those of the middle class. In contrast to the aestheticized art of the coachbuilder, the form of the Model T was an example of the body engineer's functionalist approach. The hood was a plain sheet-metal cabin protecting the engine, and the passenger compartment was essentially a wood-framed rectangular structure clad with stamped sheet-metal panels that fit together along straight edges and square corners.

By the 1920s there were four main sources for car body design. The most common were the resident body engineers employed by all the major auto manufacturers. The second, less typical source was a specialized in-house body designer or stylist with some artistic training. A third option would have been a designer from one of the coachbuilding firms under contract to develop ideas for mass-produced cars and perhaps several custom bodies for a more expensive line. But the most alluring sculptural bodies came from independent coachbuilders, either recommended by the maker or selected by the client.[4] Money was no object for society's elite, and the most talented coachbuilders had the freedom to fully express their artistic talents down to the smallest, most luxurious detail.

In the late 1920s and 1930s the newest coachbuilt designs were introduced to a receptive audience through high-profile public events like the New York,

Fig. 2. 1927 Ford Model T.

Chicago, and Paris auto salons, and such contests as the prestigious *concours d'elegance* in Paris, Nice, Cannes, and Monte Carlo, and the Villa d'Este Concorzo d'Eleganza on Lake Como in Italy. The concours d'elegance, literally a "competition of elegance," had its roots in the seventeenth-century French tradition of aristocrats parading their carriages through the parks of Paris. In the early twentieth century, this translated into a high-society affair in which wealthy owners entered their newest, most fashionable coachbuilt autos, sometimes having commissioned cars expressly for the event. The owners were often dressed in the latest couture from Paris, lending a flair of chic elegance to the occasion.[5] Giuseppe Figoni of the Parisian coachbuilding firm Figoni & Falaschi was renowned for working with couturiers to develop gowns that matched his car designs. Subsequently, contest winners and their automobiles were featured in European magazines and newspapers. These and other spectacles generated excitement among the press and the public alike, with huge crowds turning out to admire the latest designs. The big automakers took note of what appealed to visitors, realizing the importance of "styling" in predicting consumer preferences and in marketing their own product. They soon realized the merit of being associated with creative coachbuilders, whose design talents were sought to add prestige to the reputations of the auto companies.

In the early days of the automobile, the process of acquiring a coachbuilt motorcar involved a series of steps. First, the customer would visit a luxury automobile chassis manufacturer such as Duesenberg (fig. 3) or Packard in the United States, or Bugatti, Delage, or Hispano-Suiza in Europe, to procure a rolling chassis. The various makers were readily identifiable by the shapes of their radiators—one of the few mechanical parts that customarily remained visible after the addition of the body—as well as stylized logos, distinctive hood ornaments, and stamped hubcaps. Chassis manufacturers vied for the attention of wealthy customers and showcased their advanced engineering by competing in the widely publicized racing events and showing their products at the auto salons and concours d'elegance. Although these makers offered their own stylish bodies, rich clients who wanted to best their peers sought out the work of the finest coachbuilders.

Fig. 3. Duesenberg Model J chassis assembly, Duesenberg factory in Indianapolis, 1929.

After choosing a chassis, the customer would visit an independent coach-builder to request a full custom body or to discuss modifications to a limited-production catalog body. Some coachbuilders even maintained private offices at the manufacturers' posh showrooms to capture more business. For the most part, American coachbuilders worked on American chassis, while French coachbuilders worked on French chassis, and so on, although occasionally a chic European body appeared on an American chassis or vice versa. In a practice carried over from horse-drawn coaches, early autos were constructed with wooden body framing, over which thin plates of lightweight metal were hammered and finely burnished by metalsmiths to remove any evidence of unsightly seams. Painters, trimmers, and upholsterers completed the process. Over time, chassis makers began to offer in-house coachbuilding, but the most stunning automobiles were bodied by a small number of respected independents.

The coachbuilder's affluent clientele often played a decisive role in the design of their automobiles. As the Englishman R. E. Davidson described in his weekly motoring column for the *New Statesman* magazine in 1926:

> I spent a most fascinating day at the works of one of the most famous coachbuilders, who constructed bodywork for the nobility and gentry. It was quite exceptional for duplicates to be built, each model being as exclusive as Poiret frocks supplied to a comedy queen.
>
> The owner and his wife attended in state, inspected and criticized the various bodies under construction, and were followed around the works by a cortege of frock-coated executives. They finally sat down in a parlour full of brilliant leathers and painted panels to evolve a scheme. Some weeks later designs and drawings were submitted with a fat book of tapestry patterns and an estimate given in round figures, and guineas. The price accepted, the manager invited various shaggy aproned craftsmen to submit quotations in turn to him for the actual body building. Each craftsman had his own private gang, carpenters, polishers, trimmers, whom he personally engaged and paid.[6]

At a time when the ownership of an automobile was a powerful reflection of one's status in polite society, there was always demand for a bit of individual expression—something different yet still in the latest fashion. Fenders could always be designed a little longer and bodies a bit narrower or wider. Although the clientele at this level could afford to travel abroad and patronize the coachbuilder of their choice, personal preferences tended to lie along national lines, with the occasional exception. While British and American coachbuilders offered luxurious, more conservative styling, the German *Karosserien* were renowned for producing a baroque appearance as well as a look of power and speed, the Italian *carrozzerie* for their sporting bodies, and the French *carrosseries* for their flamboyance and fluid sophistication.

In the United States, those at the forefront of body design were stylists who worked for the custom coachbuilders, including such firms as Biddle & Smart, Brewster, Brunn, Dietrich, Fleetwood, Holbrook, Judkins, LaGrande, LeBaron, Locke, Murphy, Rollston, and Willoughby, among many others. At their peak, these preeminent workshops set the standard for the most fashionable designs in the American auto industry, and Hollywood celebrities, politicians, and corporate tycoons avidly sought out their creations.

The memoir of Raymond H. Dietrich, cofounder of LeBaron Carrossiers (1920–1925; later Lebaron Inc., 1925–1942) with Thomas L. Hibbard, recounted his introduction to the coachbuilding industry as an apprentice with the firm of Brewster and Company (1810–1937) in Long Island City, New York (fig. 4). One of the top coachbuilders, Brewster had established its reputation in the early nineteenth century as one of the finest makers of carriages and—beginning in 1896—automobile bodies. So well regarded was the firm that in 1934 Cole Porter immortalized it in his hit Broadway musical *Anything Goes* with Ethel Merman singing the lyrics: "You're the top! You're a Ritz hot toddy. You're the top! You're a Brewster body."

Dietrich's experience with Brewster, which began in 1913 as a "delineator," provides insight into the world of the coachbuilding guild system, in which candidates graduated from apprentice to journeyman and ultimately to master craftsman through years of experience and demonstrated talent. Dietrich's job as a delineator entailed the production of full-scale side and front elevations of the body, based on sketches by the staff designer that had been approved by the client. The drawing would include the placement of the seats and doors and any dimensions that were specified at the time of the order, but no body details or construction cross-sections. From this draft and the original designer's sketches, the master craftsman created the framework and body panels, interpreting the client's desires using his decades of experience in the business.

Fig. 4. 1934 Brewster.

Within the company, small crews of men with specialized talents worked as subcontractors on commission, following the centuries-old tradition of the coachbuilding trade. They operated independently, vying against one another for every commission. Crews were headed by a master craftsman who supervised a staff of journeymen and apprentices. Shaping and sanding was done by apprentices, while the more difficult jobs such as laminating, metal shaping, and delicate assembly were performed by journeymen. Upon the master's final approval, the body was sent to trimming and upholstery, where another group completed the job.

To ensure his livelihood, the master craftsman carefully guarded the techniques of his trade. Dietrich recalled:

During the first year of my apprenticeship, this secret method aroused my curiosity to such an extent that I visited the woodworking shop at every opportunity. It seemed odd that one of these master body builders would guard his particular method from other master body builders. Not even the apprentices employed by them were ever allowed to watch the master create his masterpiece. Each one had his own hall mark of identification which was usually burned in on the inside of the sill in much the same manner as silversmiths, makers of fine tapestries, and [makers of] furniture used to identify their work during the days of the guild systems.

Well aimed mallets sometimes ushered me out of the department but my persistence paid off. One of these masters, John Wasserman, would occasionally talk with me. His nationality and my German name were compatible, and he was amused and flattered by my interest. . . .

Men like Wasserman were intelligent, talented and highly trained. They could justify their positions. Most of them had studied as apprentices in France, England, and Germany with the top carriage and coach builders, after being graduated by the technical schools of those countries.[7]

In the United States the coachbuilding era lasted fewer than twenty years, beginning just before 1917, when the country entered World War I, and basically ending in the mid-1930s, a casualty of the Great Depression. A few firms persisted; for example, Bohman & Schwartz survived until 1940, and Derham remained in business until 1969. In Europe the practice continued on a limited basis with occasional flashes of brilliance into the early 1960s. Surviving coachbuilders continued to produce elegant bodies, but their role as industry leaders had diminished greatly. They hung on as either small shops or merely names folded into larger independent body manufacturers as an enhancement of their prestige.

The onset of the Great Depression in 1929 decimated the economies of virtually every Western country. As the calamity bottomed out in the United States in the early 1930s, morale reached a new low in the auto industry as both custom coachbuilders and luxury automakers faced bankruptcy. In the midst of the crisis, one bright spot was the 1933 Chicago World's Fair, "A Century of Progress." Among the numerous attractions that looked toward a more optimistic future, several experimental "dream cars" were exhibited. One automobile that captured the imagination of the public was the radically streamlined 1933 Pierce-Arrow Silver Arrow (see page 26), designed by Philip O. Wright (1903–1967) and crafted in the Studebaker factory in South Bend, Indiana.

Streamlining was a scientific principle that came out of the study of hydrodynamics and aerodynamics. It referred to the optimal shape of a moving body that would encounter the least amount of resistance as it passed through liquid or gas, with the goal of increasing speed. Applied first to steamships in the nineteenth century, streamlining was subsequently used on submarines, ocean liners, trains, airships, airplanes, and automobiles.[8] The most common streamlined shape was the blunt, rounded, tapering teardrop, which eventually found its way onto automobile bodies and rear fenders and came to be associated with a stylistic movement in the 1930s and 1940s.

The streamlined, aerodynamic body of the Pierce-Arrow Silver Arrow, the result of wind-tunnel tests, foreshadowed the look of future automobiles. To minimize wind resistance, the headlight moldings flowed to the tail, panels concealed the spare tires behind the front wheels, the door handles were recessed, and fully skirted rear fenders helped to reduce drag. The V-shaped motif of the grille was echoed in both the raked windshield and (upside-down) in the rear window. There were no wooden structural elements, and the roof panel was hammered from a single sheet of steel, with all the body panels welded together.

Aerodynamics dictated a rounder, more unified body with limited or no surface ornamentation, and the innovative Chrysler Airflow (1934–1937) was the first production car to incorporate the latest research into streamlining (fig. 5). In contrast to the Silver Arrow, however, the continuous, rounded form

Fig. 5. 1934 Chrysler Airflow.

of the Airflow, which broke from traditional automotive styling, was ridiculed by the public and proved to be a dismal failure in the marketplace. It seemed that consumers preferred an aestheticized aerodynamic "look" rather than a truly aerodynamic form. In an interesting twist, automotive and aeronautical engineers pointed out that the differential in power needed to overcome drag between the boxier forms of the 1920s and the streamlined ones of the 1930s was negligible. It seemed that advances in wind resistance sold better as a stylistic conceit than as a technological necessity. In 1928, American technology and architecture critic Lewis Mumford wrote:

> During the last thirty years we have become more conscious of the esthetic possibilities of the exact arts; and it is no accident that our newest instruments, the automobile and the aeroplane, are not the weakest but the best of our machine products, a distinction that they share with American kitchen equipment and bathroom fixtures. Under our very eyes, an improvement in design has taken place, transforming the awkward mass and the broken lines of the primitive auto into the unified mass and the slick stream-lines of the modern car. . . .[9]

So popular was the streamline aesthetic with the American public that designers of consumer products and architects adopted it as a decorative style. In the 1930s streamlining was applied to a broad variety of static objects (fig. 6) to make them appear modern and commercially appealing. As the American industrial designer Harold Van Doren observed in 1940:

Streamlining has taken the modern world by storm. We live in a maelstrom of streamlined trains, refrigerators, and furnaces; streamlined bathing beauties, soda crackers, and facial massages. . . . The manufacturer who wants his laundry tubs, his typewriters, or his furnaces streamlined is in reality asking you to modernize them, to find the means for substituting curvilinear forms for rectilinear forms. He wants you to make cast iron and die-cast zinc and plastics and sheet metal conform to the current taste, or fad if you will, for cylinders and spheres or the soft flowing lines of the modern automobile in place of the harsh angles and ungainly shapes of a decade ago.[10]

Fig. 6. Kem Weber (American, 1889–1963), *Armchair*, 1934, chrome-plated steel and Naugahyde upholstery, High Museum of Art, purchase with funds from the Decorative Arts Acquisition Trust, 1988.224 A–C.

Fig. 7. 1937 Horch 853 Sport Cabriolet.

Streamlining remained strong as an artistic movement well into the 1940s. In architecture it came to be called Streamline Modern—a spare, sleeker interpretation of Art Deco that was characterized by a generally horizontal orientation, rows of small windows (rectangular or round in the shape of portholes), molded stripes in shallow relief, flat roofs, smooth walls with rounded corners, metallic decorative trim, and an overall suggestion of speed or movement.

European coachbuilders also embraced the teardrop and the concept of streamlining with flamboyant styling that peaked in the late 1930s. Independent research and parallel developments in the field of aerodynamics yielded similar results but for different reasons. The new German autobahns (high-speed motorways) created great enthusiasm for streamlining, and companies such as Mercedes-Benz and Horch, a division of Auto-Union, produced elegant, high-performance automobiles for both the road (fig. 7) and the racetrack.

Fig. 8. 1938 Porsche Type 64, ca. 1939.

Porsche built a small series of streamlined racers (fig. 8) for a proposed Berlin-to-Rome race that ended up being curtailed because of the war (see page 74).

In Italy, companies such as Alfa Romeo withstood the economic depression to create some of the most beautiful road cars in the world (see page 68), while simultaneously achieving great success in the field of motor sport (fig. 9). And, as in the case of high-style fashion and luxury decorative arts, arguably the finest and most imaginative car bodies came from France. Just as the 1925 Paris Exposition Internationale des Arts Décoratifs et Industriels Modernes influenced the arts worldwide and inspired Art Deco, Paris became the center of automotive aesthetics, drawing extraordinary body designers from other nations. Masterpieces of French body design included the most revered coachbuilders and marques of the day, such as the 1937 Bugatti Type 57S Atalante by Jean Bugatti (see page 44); the 1937 Dubonnet Hispano-Suiza H-6C "Xenia" by Jean Andreau, executed by Carrosserie Saoutchik (see page 56); and the sleek, all-aluminum 1937 Delage D8-120S by Georges Paulin, realized by Carrosserie Pourtout (see page 50). The result was a collective body of work that reflected an opulent and leisured world, and the designers reveled in a luxurious form vocabulary that remains unmatched to this day.

Soon after Germany's invasion of Poland in 1939, the enthusiasm for motor racing in Europe waned as warring nations turned their attention toward the growing conflict. Automotive factories' resources and coachbuilders' talents were redirected toward the war effort. The workshops of Figoni & Falaschi in Paris, for example, were requisitioned by the French government and ordered to make components for the aircraft industry, and Scuderia Ferrari's race shop in Maranello, Italy, began manufacturing machine tools.[11] As hostilities grew worse, major European industrial centers and manufacturing plants became targets of aerial bombardment; automobile factories were hit especially hard since many had been converted to armament production. By the end of the war in 1945, the widespread destruction in Germany nearly cost that country its entire auto industry, while in Italy the return to manufacturing came slowly as shortages of building materials delayed postwar reconstruction. Financial and technological assistance came in 1948 by way of the European Recovery

Program, better known as the Marshall Plan. War-ravaged nations received billions of American dollars as well as information on the latest technological developments to help rebuild their cities and stabilize their economies. In the automotive industry, Chrysler assisted Italy's Fiat and Alfa Romeo through the establishment of subsidiary factories and by sharing new technology.

The postwar years brought about radical changes in the aesthetic of coach-built automobiles. Politics dictated the future of car design as the industry shifted away from the expansive, opulent cars of the prewar period toward smaller, faster sports cars. In both France and Italy the political power of the Communist-dominated labor unions shaped the industry in different ways. French communists were hostile toward the wealthy and therefore toward the luxury-car manufacturers. The victims of a crippling luxury tax, Bugatti, Delage, Delahaye, and Talbot-Lago were soon out of business, signaling the demise of the extravagantly detailed bespoke automobile. In Italy, the situation paralleled developments in the country's decorative arts and design industry, in which the government supported small-volume manufacturers. The 1950s saw the rise of luxurious sports cars designed by brilliant young engineers and talented coachbuilders, extending Italian supremacy in car design into the second half of the century.

The phenomenon that lifted Italy from economic devastation and secured its reputation as a source for sophisticated, high-style design—of sports cars as well as fashion, furniture, glass, ceramics, metalwork, lighting, household goods, and office machines—came to be known as the "Italian miracle." Although new, modern factories were being built to replace the ones that had been damaged or destroyed during the war, they did not displace the smaller, established, family-owned workshops that had existed for generations. A symbiotic cooperation developed instead. Since the workshops placed a premium on creativity and technical execution, they often served as laboratories where designers developed new ideas, as well as functioning as subcontractors for small-scale industrial production. New designs could be fabricated very quickly, without the need for advance planning and costly investment in new machinery. The result was an export industry of high-quality, handmade

products for a global consumer base ready to resume a more comfortable lifestyle after years of wartime austerity. In the automobile industry this translated into the nimble and elegant Italian sports car.

By the early 1950s the demand for sports cars was at an all-time high, and Italy's industry flourished. Ferrari used many coachbuilders—including the *carrozzerie* Bertone, Touring, Vignale, and Zagato—before awarding most of its work to Società Anonima Carrozzeria Pinin Farina (later Carrozzeria Pininfarina). Overseas sales were vital, with the prosperous United States becoming a key export market. Carrozzeria Ghia, like many other Italian coachbuilders, appealed to American domestic car manufacturers because of its capacity to build prototype bodies and limited runs very quickly and less expensively. During a fifteen-year partnership with Chrysler, the Ghia workshop created several exceptional car bodies, including the sporty, futuristic 1954 Dodge Firearrow III concept car (see page 92). Other international associations included

Fig. 9. 1938 Alfa Romeo wins 1948 race in Watkins Glen, New York.

Fig. 10. Preston Tucker presented his preproduction Torpedo in shows throughout the United States.

Carrozzeria Pininfarina's relationship with Nash and General Motors in the United States, with Peugeot in France, and with British Motor Corporation in England.

In the United States, following a period of postwar exuberance that included the legendary 1948 Tucker Torpedo (fig. 10 and page 80), the major automakers continued to introduce large vehicles with ornate chrome ornamentation. In response to a decline in automobile sales in the mid-1950s, American carmakers flooded the market with even larger and longer bodies with more chrome decoration. "Dynamic obsolescence caused by the annual model change," stated a 1958 General Motors paper, "is the lifeblood of the auto industry and a key factor in the national economy."[12] As if to prove this point, in 1959 the towering Cadillac tail fins reached their zenith. The American public, however, was becoming increasingly disenchanted with domestic automobiles. Consumers started demanding smaller, safer, and more fuel-efficient vehicles, and sales of quality European imports began to overtake those of domestic manufacture.

The mid-1960s marked the closing stages of the custom-built automobile with two main developments that sealed the fate of the coachbuilder. Within the industry, the widespread acceptance of unitary construction made the creation of totally personalized bodies extremely difficult. But external forces were also at work. The implementation of new safety regulations constrained the design and construction of cars worldwide. Ralph Nader's 1965 book *Unsafe at Any Speed: The Designed-In Dangers of the American Automobile* rebuked car manufacturers and called for the introduction of such features as supplemental restraint systems, five-mile-per-hour bumpers, and emission controls to ensure the safety of drivers, passengers, pedestrians, and the environment. Nader's testimony to Congress led to the 1968 National Safety and Motor Vehicle Act, which initially restricted American car design and that of European imports. The golden age of the coachbuilt automobile had come to an end.

Although a few custom coachbuilders like Pininfarina, Zagato, and Bertone survive in Italy, and several traditional coachbuilding firms are still extant in Great Britain, most of their work consists of small production runs for high-end makers like Ferrari, Aston Martin, Rolls-Royce, and Bentley.

A surprising number of elegant coachbuilt cars of the 1930s and 1940s and exclusive high-performance sports models of the 1950s and 1960s survive as prized and pampered possessions of enthusiastic collectors, who proudly exhibit their cars at lavish annual events like the Pebble Beach Concours d'Elegance in California (fig. 11) and a host of smaller but equally elegant assemblages, including the Amelia Island Concours in Florida, the Hilton Head Island Concours in South Carolina, the 100 Motor Cars of Radnor Hunt in Pennsylvania, and the Glenmoor Gathering of Significant Automobiles in Ohio. Events like the Classic Car Club of America "Caravans" and the California Mille encourage long drives, and historic races at Monterey and Lime Rock Park welcome owners who compete with enthusiasm.

At these modern concours events, vintage cars are carefully judged for authenticity, elegance, and beauty—just as they were in the 1920s—as well as restoration quality. Fashion models often accompany the cars, dressed in stylish and complementary outfits. The Pebble Beach Concours d'Elegance and the Concorzo d'Eleganza Villa d'Este at Lake Como in Italy host automotive stylists and authorities to judge an invited group of fine pre- and postwar cars that have been restored to perfection. At these events, one car is awarded the coveted Best of Show trophy, taking into consideration its styling, the beauty of its design, and the restorer's choice of authentic colors and finishes; at some events there are Best of Show awards for both a touring car and a competition car. Before they are presented, classic car owners, skilled craftsmen, and restorers carefully research these historic automobiles, often relying on period photography, company archives, and vintage coachbuilder renderings, so they can restore the cars exactly as built. Unrestored but well-preserved examples are also welcome; over-restoration is discouraged, and authenticity is praised. Over the years, a great deal has been learned about the custom design process, vintage construction techniques, color and fabric choices, and the meticulous restoration of often-complex mechanical components. The intent is to preserve and protect these cars, as collectors and museums have preserved fine art, sculpture, period architecture, costumes, and jewelry, so that generations to come can appreciate these remarkable rolling artifacts of an era that will long be remembered.

Fig. 11. 1937 Delage wins Best of Show at the 2005 Pebble Beach Concours d'Elegance.

NOTES

1. Arthur J. Pulos, *The American Design Adventure: 1940–1975* (Cambridge, Massachusetts: The MIT Press, 1988), 371.

2. Fred Horsley, *Dream Cars* (Los Angeles: Trend, Inc. Publishers, 1953), 127–130.

3. Ken Vose, "Rolling Sculpture: From Delahayes to Duesenbergs, These Stunning Cars are Tributes to the Coachbuilder's Art," http://www.cigaraficionado.com/Cigar/CA_Archives/ CA_Show_Article/0,2322,645,00.html (accessed 08/10/2009).

4 Michael Lamm, "The Beginning of Modern Auto Design," *The Journal of Decorative and Propaganda Arts* 15 (Winter–Spring 1990): 63.

5. Michael Lamm, *A Century of Automotive Style: 100 Years of American Car Design* (Stockton, California: Lamm-Morada Publishing Company, 1996), 46–47.

6. Vose, "Rolling Sculpture."

7. Mark Theobold, "Dietrich Inc. – 1925–1936 – Detroit, Michigan – Raymond H. Dietrich – 1930–1931 – New York, New York – Ray Dietrich Inc. – 1949–1953 – Grand Rapids, Michigan," *Coachbuilt*, http://www.coachbuilt.com/bui/d/dietrich/dietrich.htm (accessed 08/12/2009).

8. Kathryn B. Hiesinger, *Landmarks of Twentieth-Century Design: An Illustrated Handbook* (New York: Abbeville Press Publishers, 1993), 113–114.

9. Lewis Mumford, "Art in the Machine Age," *Saturday Review of Literature* (September 8, 1928): 102.

10. Harold Van Doren, *Industrial Design: A Practical Guide*, 9th edition (New York: The Maple Press Company, 1940), 137.

11. Warren W. Fitzgerald, Richard F. Merritt, and Jonathan Thompson, *Ferrari: The Sports and Gran Turismo Cars*, 4th edition (New York: W. W. Norton & Company, 1979), 13.

12. Pulos, *American Design Adventure*, 380.

The Automobiles

KEN GROSS

1930
Bentley Speed Six "Blue Train Special"

Chassis No. HM2855, Reg. No. GJ3811

Walter Owen Bentley, or W. O., as he was popularly called, started out as a railway locomotive apprentice, then became an aircraft engine designer. He began the production of sporting automobiles in 1919. When he learned of the 24-Hour Race at Le Mans, he entered his cars to prove the strength and durability of their designs. A Bentley won the 24-Hour "Sarthe Classic" for the first time in 1924, and before manufacture ceased in 1931, when his own firm entered receivership, Bentleys would win the grueling race four more times. Ettore Bugatti, whose cars were for the most part light and lithe, is said to have commented sarcastically, "Monsieur Bentley builds the world's fastest lorries [trucks]."

W. O. favored long-stroke, torque-rich, gear-driven, single overhead camshaft 3.0-liter and 4.5-liter 4-cylinder engines, with their cylinder heads and blocks cast as one piece to prevent gasket failures. Bentley's engines had lightweight aluminum pistons, and four valves per cylinder—all very advanced features for that era. A 6½-liter, 6-cylinder engine appeared in 1925, just as millionaire South African mining heir and financier Joel Woolf "Babe" Barnato tried to shore up the firm's finances. Although Bentley's fortunes at Le Mans sagged in 1925 and 1926, a Bentley 3-liter tourer "pipped" a French Aries in 1927 to win in the race's last hour.

Publicity from the Le Mans victories brought international acclaim to the small English firm. Bentley redesigned its 6-cylinder and introduced a powerful 180 bhp, 402.6 cid six in 1928, which was known as the Speed Six Model. Tuned versions were rated at more than 200 bhp, at just 3,500 rpm, and with them Barnato and a group of socially prominent sporting companions—who would soon become known as "The Bentley Boys"—attacked Le Mans with a vengeance. Barnato and co-driver Bernard Rubin won in 1928, and a Bentley repeated that feat for the next two years, both times with Barnato at the wheel. The five Le Mans victories proved that Bentley's utter reliability and muscular brawn could beat lighter cars with high-revving power plants.

Woolf Barnato enjoyed driving Bentleys on the road as well as on the track. A bon vivant and acknowledged ladies' man, he made the boast—probably fueled by a few cocktails—to a crowd at a party in Cannes in March 1930 that

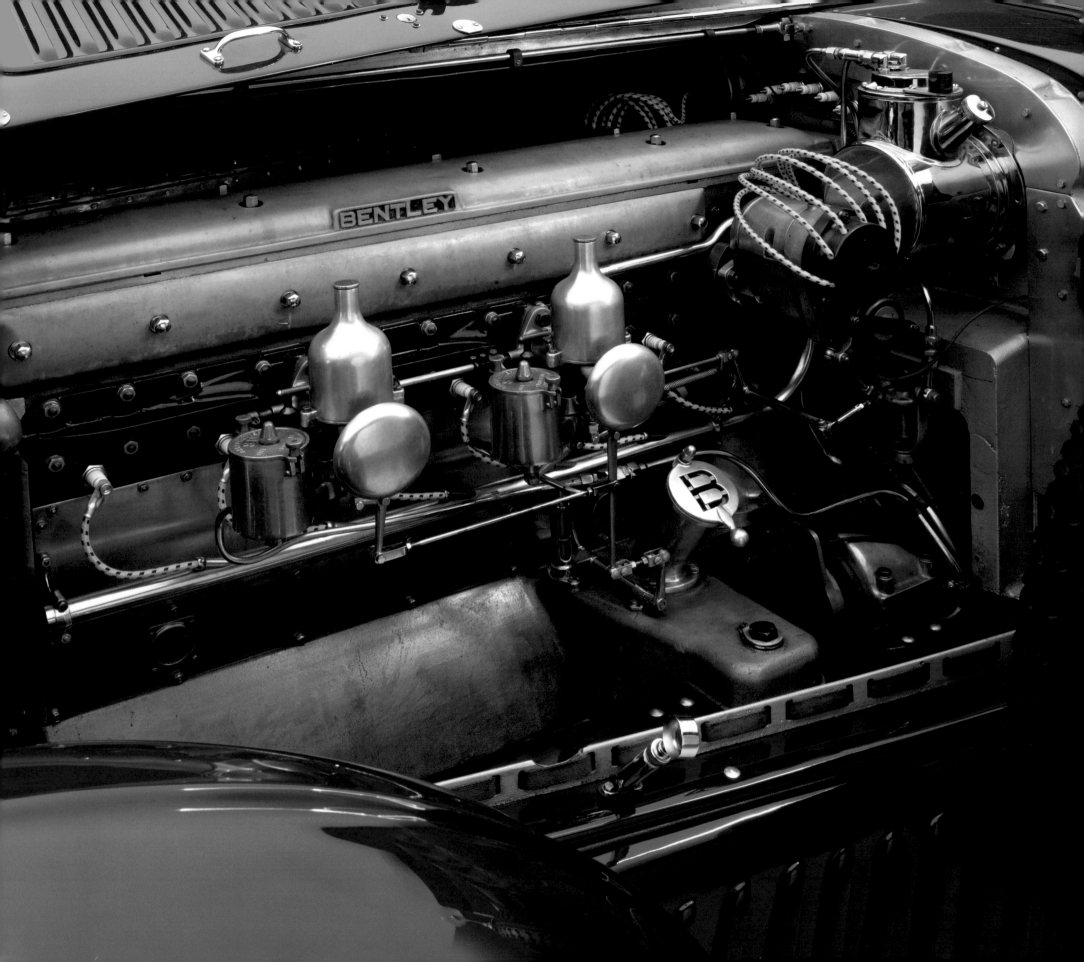

his Bentley Speed Six was faster than the much-admired "Blue Train" (*Le Train Bleu*) that ran between Cannes on the French Riviera and the port of Calais in northern France. A Rover Light Six had raced the Blue Train to Calais on public roads and beaten its time. Barnato said he would do this feat one better. He declared that he could start in Cannes at the same time as the famous train and be sitting in his club in London before the train reached Calais. Betting the then-lofty sum of 100 pounds Sterling, Barnato (with his friend Dale Bourne as relief driver) set off in his H. J. Mulliner-bodied Speed Six formal four-door saloon, just as the Blue Train left Cannes station late in the afternoon of the very next day.

Outside Lyons, traveling fast in pitch darkness, Barnato drove headlong through a heavy rainstorm. Near Auxerre, the Speed Six lost precious time while its drivers searched for a pre-arranged refueling stop. The hurtling car blew a tire outside Paris, forcing Barnato to stop and use his sole spare. Hammering the massive Bentley over narrow and unfamiliar French Routes Nationales in the dark, the intrepid duo reached the coast at 10:30 the next morning, boarded a cross-Channel packet ferry, and were parked in front of

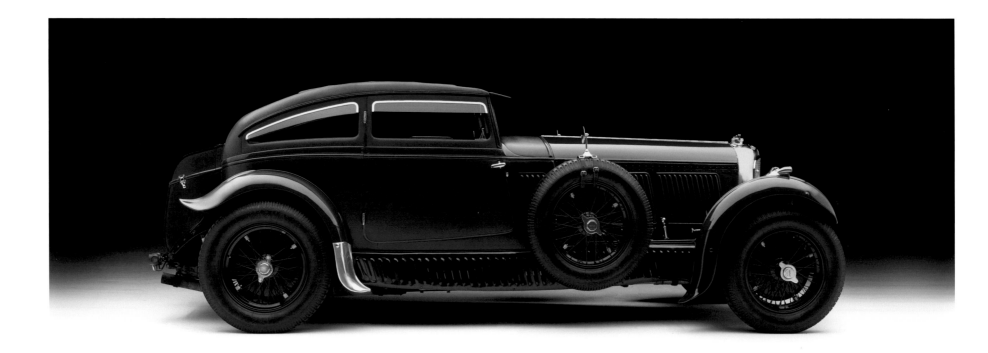

The Conservative Club in St. James Street, London, by 3:30 p.m., precisely four minutes before the Blue Train arrived in Calais. Barnato had won the bet, but when news of his daredevil stunt was made public he was fined by indignant French authorities—and reportedly had to pay a sum far greater than his winnings—for unauthorized racing on public highways.

In May 1930, Barnato took delivery of a J. Gurney-Nutting and Co.-bodied, semi-streamlined "Sportsman Coupe." Barnato named this one-of-a-kind car "The Blue Train Special" to commemorate his driving feat. It soon became known as the "Blue Train Bentley," even though it was not believed to be the actual car that had raced the train. A fanciful commemorative painting showing this coupe racing *Le Train Bleu* and several historic written accounts added to the confusion over time. The Blue Train Bentley Speed Six's saloon bodywork was removed and replaced, making matters worse. The late Diana Barnato Walker, Woolf Barnato's daughter, always insisted that the Gurney-Nutting coupe had been delivered earlier and that it was indeed the car in which her father raced the Blue Train. Perhaps we shall never know for certain, but it should be noted that Bentley Motors—in commemoration of the 75th anniversary of the famous race—brought both cars to France to retrace the route and used the outline of the coupe on the plaque of the "Blue Train Edition" Arnage.

Barnato's Gurney-Nutting fastback was distinguished by its mean, purposeful look, thanks to its dramatically low roofline, a leatherette Weymann-style lightweight body with a built-in trunk and tool kit, louvered chassis valences, rakishly flared cycle fenders, and tall wire wheels. It was the perfect transport for the well-known sportsman who exemplified the dashing spirit of Bentley. The coupe could accommodate three passengers, but its single rear seat was placed sideways because of the car's low roofline. Some have speculated that rear compartment—with its small cocktail cabinet and the sideways seat—was designed for the occasional dalliance.

After Barnato, the Gurney-Nutting coupe was owned by Lord Brougham and Vaux; later it was the property of Charles Mortimer, a famed Brooklands Outer Bank racing driver. Stored haphazardly in a Midlands timber garage, it fell into disrepair until it was restored by Hugh Harben, who did most of the work himself, modifying the engine and braking system and adding a Webasto folding sunroof. The present owners of this storied Gurney-Nutting coupe also purchased the original "Blue Train Bentley" saloon as well as the car with the original body, and have reunited the two pieces. They now possess both of these famous Woolf Barnato Bentley cars. This car is lent by Bruce and Jolene McCaw of Seattle, Washington.

GJ 3811

1931
Duesenberg SJ Convertible Sedan

Engine No. SJ-488

The Duesenberg, known as "America's Mightiest Motor Car," was built by the Auburn-Cord-Duesenberg Company in Auburn, Indiana. Erret Lobban Cord, a renowned entrepreneur who had been featured on the cover of *Time* magazine twice in a two-year period, was the force behind the marque. Earlier, Cord had rescued the Auburn Automobile Company, and later he offered a dramatically low-slung front-drive luxury car under his own name. In his effort to create the finest motorcar in America, Cord turned to two skilled German immigrant brothers from Indianapolis, Fred and August Duesenberg. They had built race cars that won the Indianapolis 500, pioneered supercharging, and from 1920 to 1927 they sold the Duesenberg Model A, the first American production car with four-wheel hydraulic brakes.

Funded by Cord's millions, the Duesenberg Model J was introduced at the 1928 New York Automobile Salon. The cars were very favorably received, despite a chassis price tag of $8,500; coachbuilt bodies would more than double that price. The rich and famous immediately lined up, checkbooks in hand. Sadly, Cord's timing could not have been worse. The stock market crash in October 1929 and the Great Depression that followed would soon put most luxury makes out of business. But while it lasted, the Duesenberg J (and later JN and SJ models) was magnificent. The engine was a race-inspired, polished aluminum, 265 bhp, double-overhead-cam, 32-valve straight-8 that displaced a whopping 420 cid. These immense motors built by Lycoming, known for its aircraft power plants, were all painted green. Duesenberg claimed an astonishing 320 bhp for the Model J's successor, the supercharged Model SJ. Although actual power outputs may have been a bit less, nothing in its era could touch a seriously driven Duesenberg.

About 480 examples were completed from 1929 to 1937, although the factory and many custom coachbuilders rebodied, updated, and resold a number of individual cars (a not uncommon practice at the time for luxury makes), making it appear as though as many as 500 examples were produced. Duesenberg bodies were built by every major American coachbuilder and by numerous European *carrossiers* as well. Duesenberg owners, the crème de la crème of society, industry, politics, and show business, included candy magnates

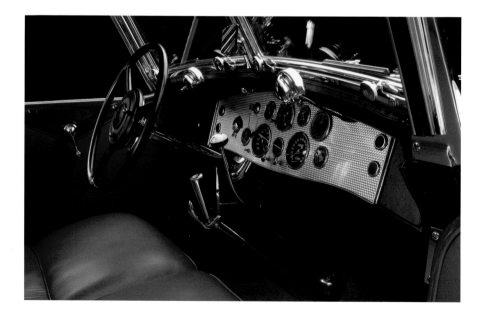

Phillip K. Wrigley and Ethel V. Mars, Josiah K. Lilly of pharmaceutical fame, and art collector and ambassador William A. M. Burden, as well as Col. Jacob Schick and W. H. Luden, who had made fortunes in razor blades and cough drops, respectively. Jimmy Walker, New York's madcap mayor, cruised Manhattan in a silk-upholstered Duesenberg limousine. (Not to be outdone, Jersey City mayor Frank Hague had two Duesies.) Walker's swanky chariot cost $20,000 in an era when families waited in breadlines and ex-bankers sold apples on street corners. Putting it in perspective, in 1929 a new Ford Model A roadster was $450.

Duesenberg's impressive social register included Horace Dodge, Cornelius Vanderbilt Whitney, and John Wanamaker, Jr. Hollywood stars Clark Gable, Joe E. Brown, Tyrone Power, Greta Garbo, and Gary Cooper all drove Duesies. Dancer Bill "Bojangles" Robinson commissioned a Rollston-bodied sedan. Col. H. H. Rogers of Standard Oil ordered a supercharged town car. Col. E. R.

Bradley, owner of the Kentucky Derby, had to be content with three Duesenbergs: a Rollston town car complemented by two limousines, one by Judkins, the other by Willoughby. The best-remembered Duesenberg print ads in *Vogue* and *Vanity Fair* never showed an actual car. There was simply a sketch of an elegant man or woman—hunting pheasants, addressing the gardener, sitting in a high, paneled library—with a single line of copy: "He (or She) drives a Duesenberg." Little wonder that the greatest custom coachbuilders of the day fought for design commissions.

Noted Duesenberg collectors included the late John O'Quinn in Texas, who owned more than a dozen examples. Former *Tonight Show* host Jay Leno owns eight Duesenbergs, including a bare Model J chassis that he fitted with a seat so it can be driven on the street. Leno also owns an unrestored 1927 Model X (a briefly built successor to the Model A) that he rescued from a Burbank garage where it had rested undisturbed since 1946. "I love Duesenbergs,"

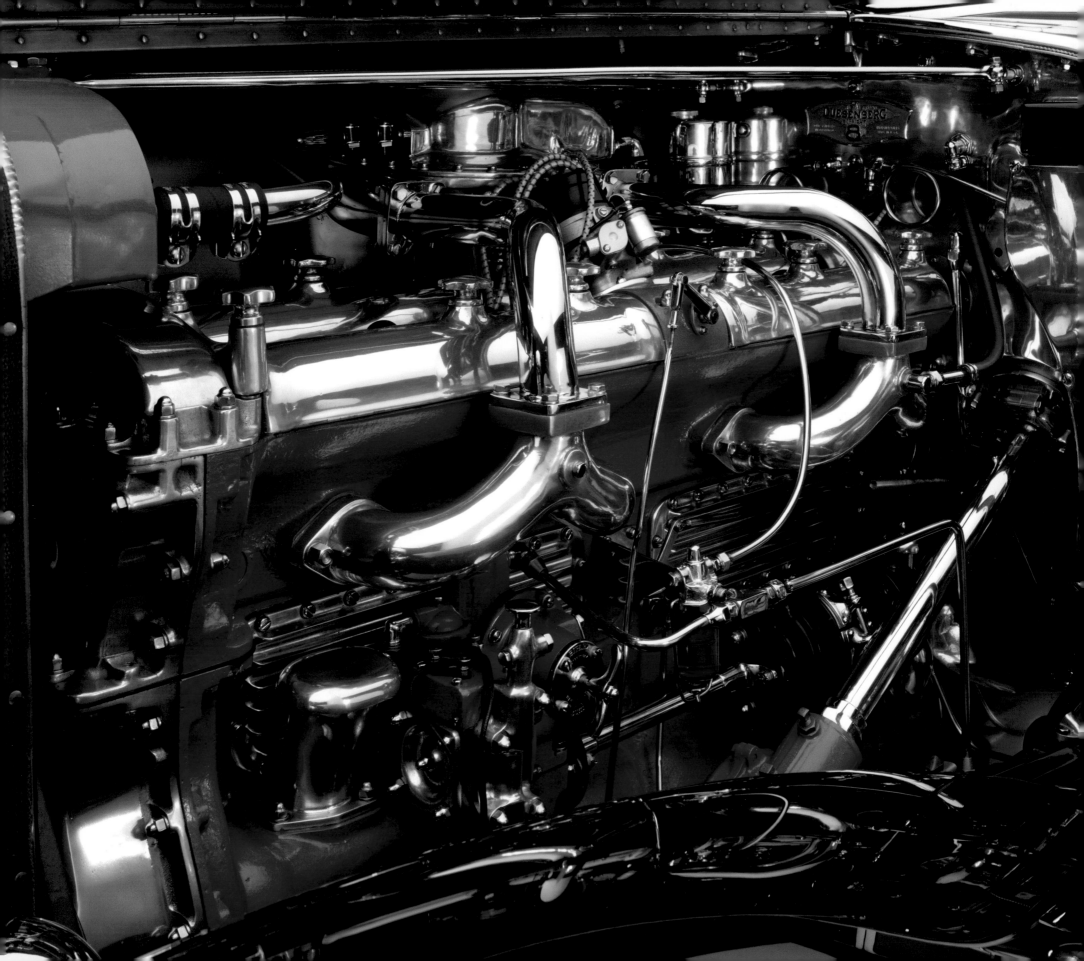

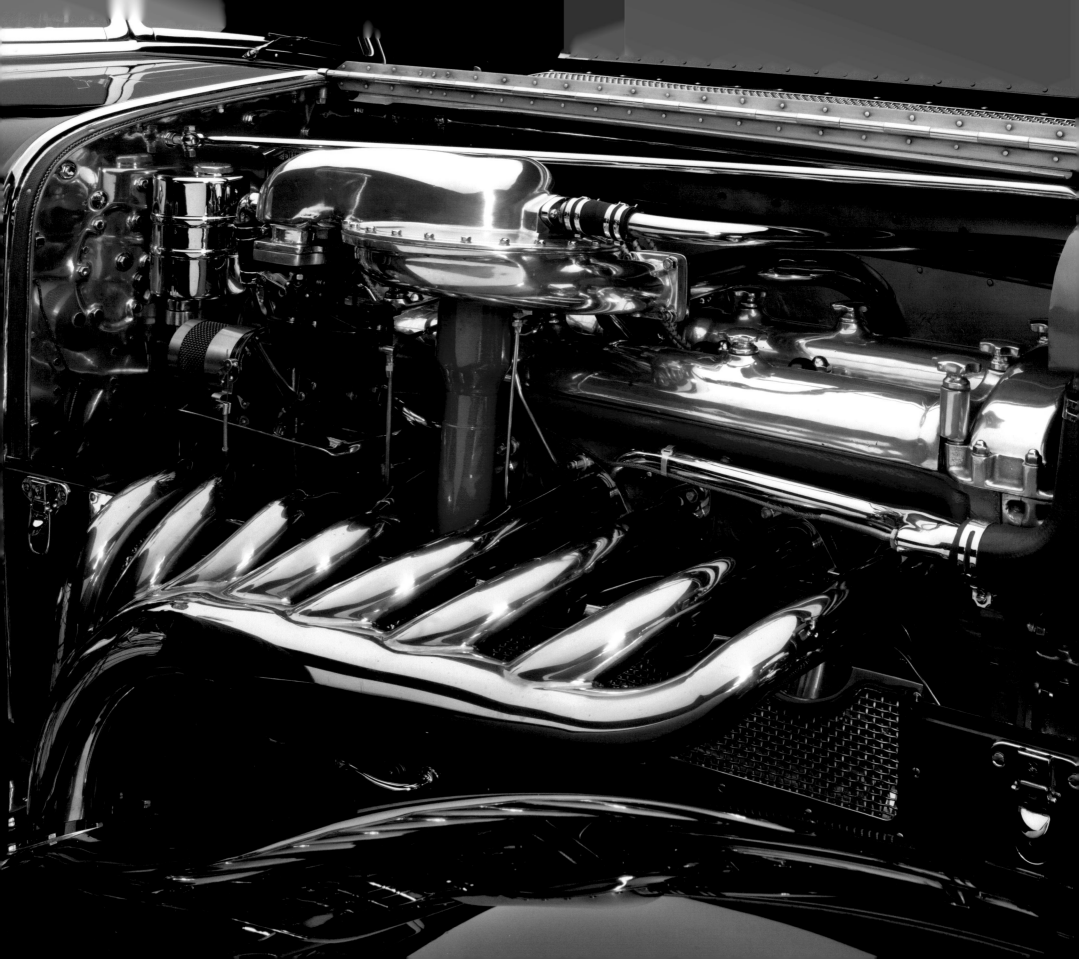

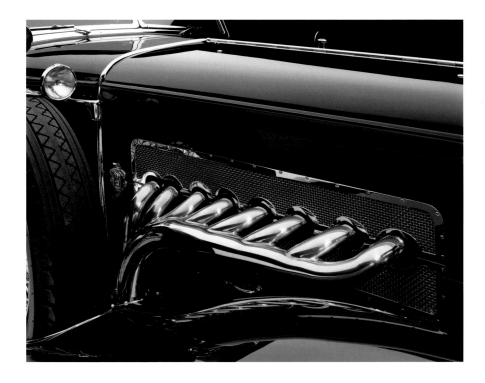

Clark Gable with his 1935 Duesenberg convertible coupe.

says Leno. "They were the first American car to beat the Europeans at their own game. Fine cars of that era were mostly lumbering limousines with slow-revving engines. Duesenbergs had high-revving, four-valve, double-overhead-cam straight-8s. They were the fastest American cars until the Chrysler 300 letter series in the mid-'50s."

This sporty short-wheelbase, split-windshield, Convertible Sedan SJ-488, chassis No. 2506, designed by Gordon Buehrig, was one of just five examples built by the Derham Body Company of Rosemont, Pennsylvania. The custom body was sold directly to the Duesenberg factory by Derham. Historian Raymond Loe noted this was not the usual practice, as most Series J's were sold as a "chassis only." Typically, purchasers then contracted separately with coachbuilders for custom-built designs. Duesenberg expert Randy Ema believes SJ-488 was used as a factory demonstrator before being sold to its first owner, Alexander Tiers. The price was $15,250. It then passed to Dick "Hal" Rossen, who was briefly married to actress Jean Harlow.

The next owner was James Talmadge of Twentieth Century Fox, whose father was Buster Keaton. Warton Bryson, who followed Talmadge, sold it to James Strohecker of Portland, Oregon, in 1947. He owned four Duesenbergs, including a twin to this car, and was a scion of the family who owned the posh Strohecker grocery stores, which dated back to 1902. Strohecker bequeathed SJ-488 to his close friend Charles F. Norris, who kept it for thirty years before selling it to the present owners. This car has been extensively restored, but the body was never taken off the chassis. In addition to the factory supercharger, which raises the output to a claimed 320 bhp, this car has a rare one-piece, eight-port, external exhaust pipe.

Today, with auction prices for many examples exceeding seven figures, it is clear that E. L. Cord and the prolific Duesenberg brothers created a legend. People who have never heard the name Duesenberg use the expression, "It's a Duzy!" to refer to something spectacular—an enduring tribute to this classic among classics. SJ-488 was lent by Tom and Susan Armstrong, Issaquah, Washington.

1933
Pierce-Arrow Silver Arrow

Pierce-Arrow was descended from Heintz, Pierce and Munschauer, a company founded in 1865 that manufactured bird cages and iceboxes in Buffalo, New York. When George N. Pierce took control in 1896, the firm was producing bicycles. In 1901, the Pierce Motorette was produced in small volume and David Fergusson, a talented British-born engineer, signed on. Success in the challenging Glidden Tour soon followed, along with a progression of ever larger, more luxurious, and more expensive Arrow and Great Arrow models. Advanced features such as column-mounted shifters and headlights that were faired into the front fenders marked Pierce's progress. The company soon became the darling of very wealthy owners. With its dignified advertising, elegant if a bit stodgy styling, and legion of respectable dealers, Pierce rivaled Packard for prestige.

Pierce-Arrow pioneered the extensive use of aluminum, including cast-aluminum bodies, and was the first to feature hydraulic valve operation. But the ultra-conservative marque persisted with right-hand drive until 1920 and its cars, save for their unusual (and patented) modern headlamp treatment, clung to six-cylinder engines long after Cadillac and Packard turned to more powerful and smoother V-8s and Twin-Sixes. Despite the company's reputation for quality, and even with the introduction of four-wheel hydraulic brakes in 1926, Pierce sales diminished and the company was forced to merge with plebian Studebaker. The resulting new Pierce straight-8 was moderately successful, but the 1929 stock market crash telegraphed a dire warning that at first went unheeded. Under new chief engineer Karl Wise, Pierce produced a powerful V-12 that temporarily upstaged its rivals and set numerous stock car speed records on the Bonneville Salt Flats in the capable hands of the endurance racer Ab Jenkins.

Desiring to rationalize the look of its car lines, despite pricing and dimensional differences, Pierce and Studebaker offered two body styles in common, and this led to a heroic joint project in the dark days of 1932. Philip O. Wright, a talented stylist for the Walter L. Murphy Company, who had earlier designed the snappy L-29 Cord Speedster, presented a design proposal for a streamlined fastback luxury two-door body with racy pontoon fenders on the Pierce V-12

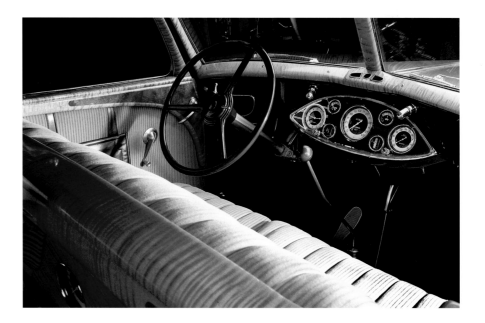

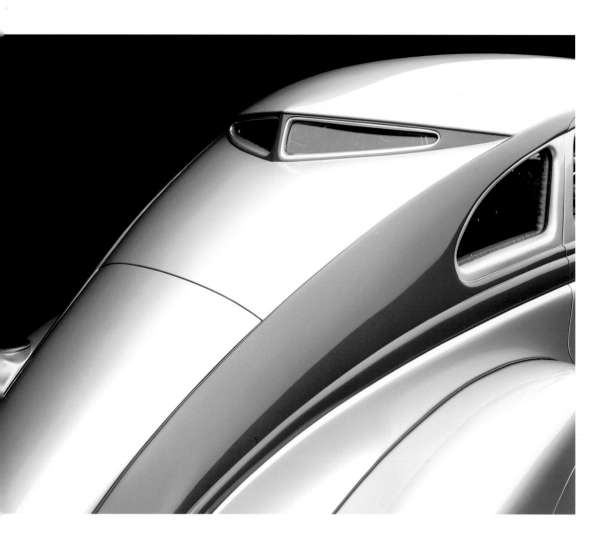

Chassis. Pierce-Arrow vice-president Roy Faulkner loved it. Wright moved to the Studebaker headquarters in South Bend, Indiana, where he worked alongside Studebaker's body designer James Hughes, who had trained at Rolls-Royce, Renault, and Lincoln. Under Hughes's influence, Phil Wright's rakish design evolved into a sporty four-door sedan with a smart low roofline and rounded door openings. The pontoon front fenders were discarded. Revolutionary envelope front fenders, with faired-in headlight nacelles that imitated Pierce's famous fender-mounted headlamp treatment, dramatically swept upward across the car's beltline and flowed in a graceful arc to the rear of the car. The resulting all-of-a-piece fender design would soon influence nearly every rival on the road. The streamlined sedan's straight body sides omitted traditional running boards and concealed twin spare tires. Pontoon rear fenders were fully skirted, and the old-fashioned wire wheels were covered with spun alloy discs.

Both Hughes and Wright were single-minded and strong-willed: they apparently did not work well together. Hughes reworked Wright's original rear window from a sloping, flush-mounted opening to a twin-triangular, Stream-line Modern, razor-slit glass area that was as small and impractical as it was memorable. Hughes was convinced that the narrow window would reduce glare during night driving, but the resulting opening was so tiny that it was nearly useless for rearward vision. That said, in a sea of boxy early 1930s sedans, the sexy, streamlined Pierce show car was as modern as tomorrow.

Five hand-built cars named the Silver Arrow were assembled in South Bend, and the first one was delivered to New York City on January 1, 1933. Four more Silver Arrows toured the country from one auto show to another, causing a sensation wherever they were shown. Equipped with a giant 462 cid (cubic-inch displacement) V-12 that developed 175 bhp, a Silver Arrow could top 115 mph with ease, and one of them served as the pace car for the 1933 Indy 500. Pierce exhibited at the Chicago Century of Progress Exhibition, vying with the limited-production Cadillac Aero-Dynamic Coupe, Duesenberg's "Twenty Grand," and Packard's "Car of the Dome." The Silver Arrow upstaged them all with its audacious good looks, its integrated body and fenders, and its tapered, aircraft-like shape.

Tentatively priced at a heady $10,000, the Silver Arrow was one of thirty-eight different models that Pierce-Arrow nominally offered in 1933, on four different wheelbases. But the company sold just 2,152 units in total that year, about 500 fewer than 1932 and about 1,000 cars below the break-even point. As it was for so many manufacturers in the depths of the Depression, the handwriting was on the wall for Pierce. A decision was made not to produce any more of the Pierce-Arrow show cars. For 1934, both Pierce and Studebaker marketed practical production versions of the Silver Arrow. Studebaker's effort was called the Skyway Land Cruiser, and its features included a swept-back cabin, flowing reveals, and shrouded rear wheels. Pierce-Arrow called its production streamliner the Silver Arrow, but with its dowdy side-mount spares, exposed running boards, and open rear wheels, it erased Wright's brave peek into the future and did not approach the show car's dramatic appearance.

Earlier, Wright had proposed an even more dramatic Silver Arrow successor, to be called the Golden Arrow. Extensively streamlined, it would have had a more refined chassis with independent front suspension. But Pierce-Arrow was undergoing reorganization and refinancing attempts, funds were tight, sales were shrinking, and the idea was stillborn. Pierce-Arrow clung to life until mid-1938. At the end, despite being the only American luxury carmaker to offer a Warner gear four-speed overdrive transmission with a reworked 385 cid V-12, Pierce-Arrow, a grand old automotive marque that had begun at the turn of the century, faded to oblivion. A brand famous for its conservative approach, Pierce-Arrow remains best remembered for the magnificent Silver Arrow. This example, one of three survivors, is lent by Don Williams and the Blackhawk Collection of Danville, California.

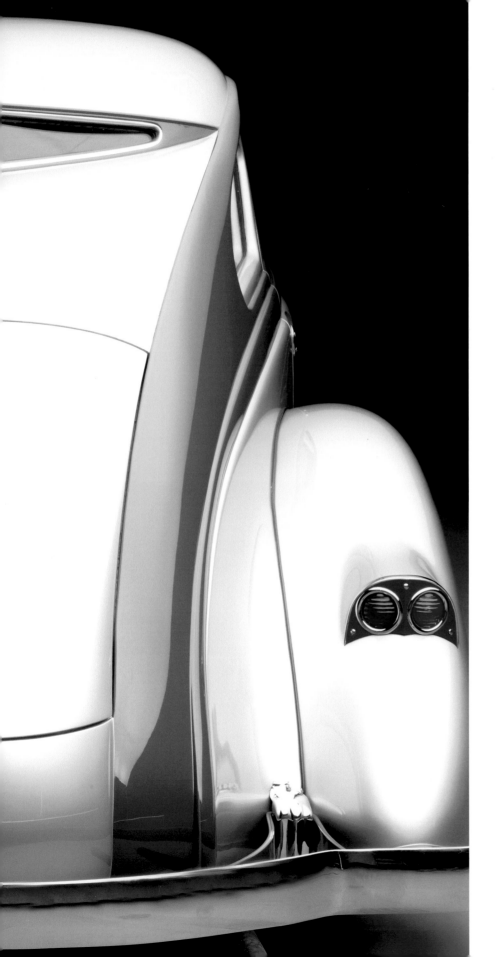

Aviation legend Eddie Rickenbacker with Harlan Fengler, the official starter of the Indianapolis Motor Speedway, next to the Pierce-Arrow Silver Arrow that served as pace car for the 1933 Indy 500.

1937
Bugatti Type 57S Atalante

CHASSIS NO. 57562

Ettore Bugatti was a mildly eccentric, egotistic Italian engineer who lived most of his life on a baronial estate in Alsace-Lorraine in eastern France. His father Carlo was an important furniture designer who produced exotic interpretations of the Art Nouveau style. His younger brother Rembrandt was an accomplished sculptor of animals. Ettore Bugatti, trained as an apprentice engineer, possessed the soul of an artist. From 1911 to 1939 Bugatti built automobiles of uncompromised elegance and sporting competence. Often technically (some would say perversely) complex, Bugatti's cars were expensive, temperamental, and—in the case of the Type 57SC Atlantic and its Grand Touring companion, the Type 57S Atalante—hauntingly beautiful.

The firm competed successfully in Grand Prix and sports car racing until the start of World War II. Bugatti experimented with aerodynamics and the use of lightweight metals such as magnesium. Known as Le Patron (the Boss), Bugatti favored expensive, self-adjusting de Ram shock absorbers. But he could also be conservative. He eschewed supercharging at first, and clung to cable-operated brakes long after hydraulics had proved superior.

Due to France's high tariffs and restricted trade, the Great Depression of 1929 was slow to affect the country. But by the early 1930s the luxury automobile market had dwindled. Ettore and his son Jean knew that it was vital to produce a special model if their company was to survive. The Type 57 was that car. Its styling was contemporary, and custom coachwork was available for those with means.

The Type 57 Atlantic, the inspiration for the later Atalante, made its debut at the 1935 Paris and London Motor Shows. Initially called the Competition

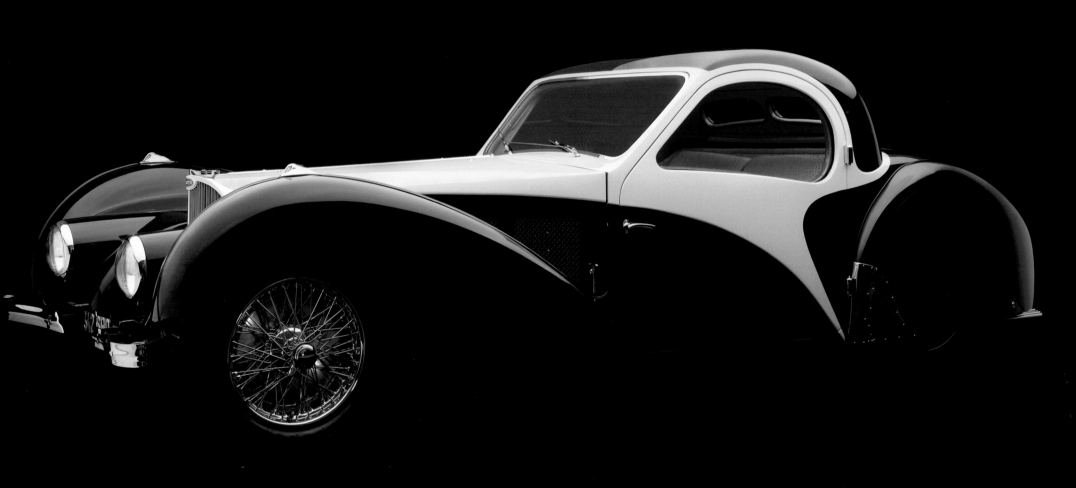

Coupe Aerolithe (French for "meteor"), it rode on a prototype Type S (for sports) chassis with gondola-shaped frame rails that tapered rearward for an aerodynamic appearance, and it was powered by a normally aspirated, 3.3-liter, dual-overhead-cam straight-8. Although other makers experimented with aerodynamic models—the sinister Mercedes-Benz Autobahn-Kurier and Talbot-Lago's voluptuous Teardrop coupes are two fine examples—nothing on the road in that era was as outrageous as the Bugatti Type 57. The curvaceous Aerolithe was a design sensation. Orders for copies were not overwhelming, but the point was made—Bugatti remained a contender.

The Atlantic was to be fabricated from Electron, a magnesium and aluminum alloy. That metal proved difficult to weld, so Jean Bugatti, assisted by Joseph Walter, used rivets to join the major sections. A spinelike center rib divided the car's svelte body—a theme repeated in its teardrop-shaped fenders. Production Atlantics were hand-fabricated in aluminum. The rivets were no longer needed, but they looked exotic, so the illusion of a riveted spine was retained. Close-coupled, cramped, poorly ventilated, and impractical, the sexy lightweight coupe was an enthusiast's delight, and one of only a handful of sports cars that could top 130 mph in its era. Four Atlantics were built, and only three survive.

For racing, a normally aspirated, 3.3-liter, straight-8-powered Type 57 on an ultra-low "S" chassis was fitted with streamlined open coachwork. The factory proudly advertised its successes, which included averaging 135.45 mph for one hour, 123.8 mph for 2,000 miles, and 124.6 mph for 4,000 kilometers. An avid horseman, Le Patron was convinced automobile competition improved the breed, just as did thoroughbred racing. Enhancing the exquisite lines of the Aerolithe-inspired Atlantic, Jean Bugatti designed the Atalante, a slightly larger, more comfortable production Grand Tourer on the Type 57 chassis. Its name was derived from Atalanta, the seductive huntress and princess of ancient Greek mythology who swore she would only marry a man who could run fast enough to catch her. The Bugatti Atalante was substantially more successful than the Atlantic, and about forty were built on the standard Type 57 and the low-slung, slightly shorter and sporting Type 57S chassis before World War II halted all production.

Normally aspirated Type 57s were rated at 135 bhp; the supercharged Type 57C was conservatively rated at 160 bhp, with three to four pounds of boost. The Type 57S, normally aspirated but with increased compression and lightweight pistons, reached 175 bhp, and the Type 57SC, incorporating the S improvements, with lower compression ratio and higher boost, developed 220 to 230 bhp. Bugatti's supercharged straight-8 is a surprisingly powerful engine. The long shift lever has a very short travel. Throttle response is immediate, and the gear-driven overhead cams whirr and click with a delightful metallic cacophony. The exhaust snarls with authority, and despite its advanced age, narrow tires, and stiff suspension, the low-slung Type 57S accelerates briskly and corners smartly. Elegant Jaeger instruments on a polished wood fascia feature long, slender needles that wave like a conductor's wand. Still nimble, the Bugatti feels like a thoroughbred—and appears to be a car that is much younger.

This curvaceous Type 57S Atalante coupe, chassis number 57562, was delivered in September 1937 by Friderich, the Bugatti agent in Nice, to the Belgian pilot Gabriel Duhoux. Next owned by Jean de Debbeleer, a famous Belgian Bugatti purveyor, it was sequestered during the war. After hostilities ended, it passed through owners in Boston, Massachusetts, and Caracas, Venezuela, then returned to France, and subsequently went to Noel Thompson in Vernon, New Jersey, from whom it was purchased by its present owner. Restored in 1996 to its original color scheme of black with yellow accents, it was shown at the Pebble Beach Concours d'Elegance that year and placed second in class.

The Type 57S Atalante is a sports car for the ages. Esteemed automotive writer Ken W. Purdy called Bugatti "the Prince of Motors." "Imagine a string-straight, poplar-lined Route Nationale in France on a summer's day," Purdy wrote. "That growing dot in the middle distance is a sky-blue Bugatti coupe rasping down from Paris to Nice at 110 miles an hour." This car is lent by William E. (Chip) Connor II, of Deepwater Bay, Hong Kong.

The Bugatti Type 57S in front of former owner Jean de Debbeleer's garage in Belgium in the 1950s.

1937
Dubonnet Hispano-Suiza H-6C "Xenia"

Andre Dubonnet, France's aperitif baron, was born in 1897. After serving as a fighter pilot in World War I in the French Air Force's "Stork" squadron (he was credited with five kills), he made his fortune producing fortified wines, one of which, flavored with arrowroot, became an international aperitif classic. An enthusiastic amateur racing driver and prolific inventor, Dubonnet (working with a little-known engineer named Antoine-Marie Chedru) developed and patented a clever independent front-suspension system in 1927. Dubonnet's invention mounted each front wheel on a single arm that extended forward from the kingpin, the main pivot in the steering mechanism. A pair of oil-filled, coil-spring cylinders offered resistance and swiveled as each wheel turned. Just the arm itself moved with wheel deflections, so the car's unsprung-weight was reduced, improving ride and handling. In 1934 General Motors

adopted a variation of this system for its Chevrolet and Pontiac brands, and Scuderia Ferrari used it on the prewar Alfa Romeo Tipo B racecar, helping to make Dubonnet even wealthier.

Dubonnet enthusiastically raced Bugattis and drove a Duesenberg in the 1921 French Grand Prix, but Hispano-Suiza automobiles were his favorites. He commissioned several showy tulipwood-bodied, copper-riveted boat-tail speedsters on Hispano chassis. Another of his stylistic creations with a very low four-door sedan body was exhibited by Hispano-Suiza, along with a bare H-6B chassis, at the 1932 Paris Salon. After the show, Dubonnet acquired that chassis and took it to the Parisian custom coachbuilder Jacques Saoutchik. The plan was to build a striking aerodynamic coupe for Dubonnet's personal use.

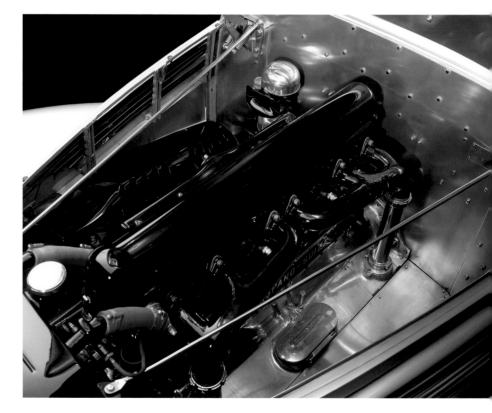

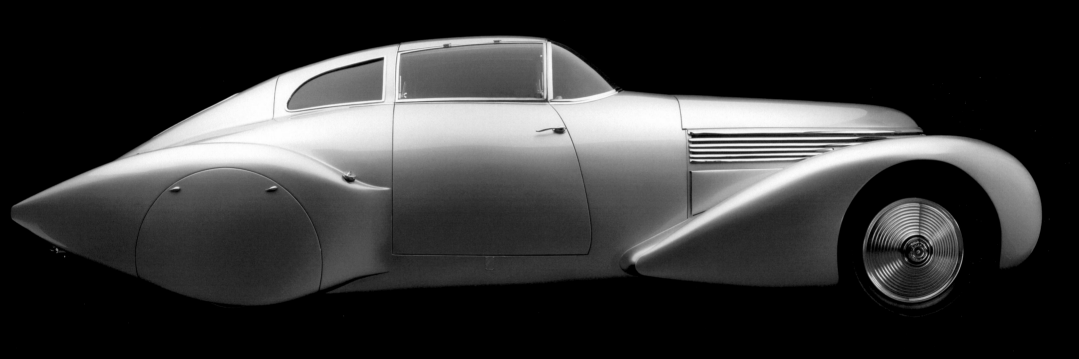

Intended as a rolling showcase for Dubonnet's ideas, the car was designed by Jean Andreau, who was known for his avant-garde streamlined aircraft and automotive creations. The one-of-a-kind construction made extensive use of curved glass in all of the windows. Its most memorable features include a panoramic windscreen (not seen again until General Motors cars in the 1950s) and plexiglass side windows that opened upward in gullwing fashion. Two extraordinary side doors, suspended on large hinges and built in parallelogram style, opened rearward in "suicide" fashion.

The long, gently rounded body resembled the fuselage of an airplane. Its slender shape tapered toward a pointed tail. The dramatic fastback was crowned with a Streamline Modern, triangular rear window. Small removable panels, set into the forward part of the roof, could be lifted out and stowed inside. The cockpit was reminiscent of then-contemporary aircraft, with a flat floor, multiple round white-on-black gauges centered between two glove boxes, and foldable bucket seats. The car was built for four passengers, thanks to a narrow rear seat for two. Clean and crisp, with no plated trim to speak of and boasting an aerodynamically efficient underside, this car scarcely resembled the flamboyant, chrome-encrusted coachwork that Saoutchik usually produced.

The engine was a Hispano-Suiza H-6B 6.5-liter overhead-valve inline-6. Capable of 144 bhp in standard form, this power plant may have been modified to the H-6C's output of 200 bhp—historians are not certain. Hood vents that cooled the large engine are reminiscent of those on an 810/812 Cord; it is theorized that Dubonnet may have seen Cord designer Gordon Buehrig's patents. The vertical slots on either side of the pointed hood also help release trapped air. The Hispano's tall and massive wire wheels are concealed by spun-alloy wheel discs embossed with elegant concentric circular ribs, and the pontoon-shaped rear fenders are smartly skirted.

Dubonnet's "Xenia" coupe emerged from the war complete and unscathed.

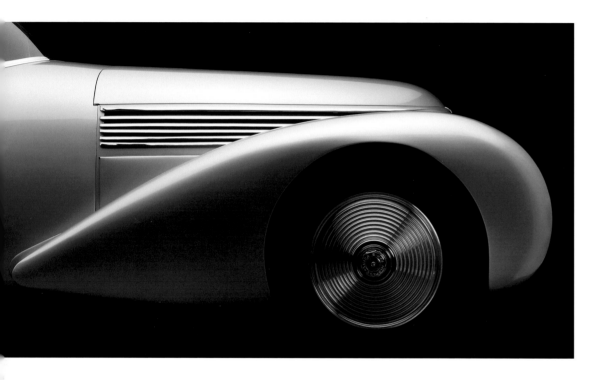

Along with a heavily reinforced chassis, this car featured Dubonnet's own hyperflex suspension system. According to French-car authorities Richard Adatto and Diana Meredith, Dubonnet claimed the new suspension would give his car "the suppleness of a cat." (He used the image of a leaping cat as his corporate logo.) Completed in 1938, with fully independent suspension on all four wheels, the coupe was said to be capable of 125 mph. Dubonnet named his creation "Xenia," after his late wife Xenia Johnson, who had died at a young age a few years before. It is said that his second wife took a dim view of the car's haunting and sentimental name.

In 1939, after World War II had begun, the Xenia was hidden away, and it was not seen in public again until June 1946, when it was photographed at the opening of the St. Cloud tunnel near Paris. It was owned in the 1950s by Raymond Aussibal of Paris, and was purchased in the 1960s by Alain Balleret, then president of the French Hispano-Suiza Club, who initiated the

car's restoration. The work was completed by Charles Morse, the Xenia's next owner, and it was shown at the Pebble Beach Concours d'Elegance in 2000. The Xenia is currently owned by Peter Mullin, a California-based collector of classic French cars.

The original Hispano-Suiza chassis sat rather high off the ground, and the Xenia was built atop the frame, so while its overall appearance is sleek and elegant, it is nonetheless a tall and heavy car. In the context of its era, the stunning Xenia was dramatically different from any of its contemporaries. It still exudes a "concept car" look, and appears to be far more modern in conception than almost any 1930s-era design. As Adatto and Meredith noted, "Long, wide and massive, with a cockpit clearly inspired by aircraft practice, the Dubonnet Hispano-Suiza evokes yesterday's vision of the future." This car is lent by Merle and Peter Mullin and the Peter Mullin Automotive Museum Foundation, Beverly Hills, California.

1937
Mercedes-Benz 540K Special Roadster

Before World War II, Daimler-Benz, parent company of automaker Mercedes-Benz, was Germany's leading producer of luxury cars and heavy trucks. The engineers at the Stuttgart-based firm were very successful in the International Grand Prix and Sports Car competitions—thanks to generous National Socialist government subsidies—employing such technology as supercharging, fully independent suspension, light-alloy metallurgy, and overhead camshafts in its road-going machines.

Beginning in 1932 with the 3.8-liter 380K, overhead-valve straight-8 ("K" stood for *Kompressor*, or supercharger), Mercedes-Benz produced a line of large, fast, grand touring cars. At the 1933 Berlin Motor Show, the 500K Autobahn-Kurier—its displacement increased from 3.8 to 5.0 liters—was offered with striking, aerodynamic fastback-coupe coachwork. A crankshaft-driven Roots-type supercharger blew the compressed fuel-air charge through a single updraft carburetor, adding 65 bhp for short periods of time when the throttle was fully depressed, engaging the "blower" and producing a shrill scream. Other motorists no doubt cringed as a hard-driven 540K howled past

them on the autobahn. The 540K had presence, panache, and power, and it still exudes those qualities today.

Although the 500K's engine produced some 160 bhp, this model's massive, truck-like ladder-frame chassis, with box-section side members and relatively heavy enclosed bodywork, needed even more power. The displacement of the cast-iron monobloc engine (its block and cylinder head were cast in one piece) was again increased, this time to 5.4 liters, producing the 180 bhp supercharged 540K model offered from 1936 to 1938. Twin exhaust pipes, enclosed in chrome-plated flexible sheaths, protruded through the sides of the hood, adding to an appearance of raw power.

Advanced for its era, the 540K's front suspension consisted of independent, unequal-length wishbones and coil springs; the rear end featured an independent, coil-sprung swing axle. The transmission was a semi-automatic four-speed (functioning automatically on the top two gears), and the 540K's oversized hydraulic drum brakes were servo-assisted. The 540K was engineered by Gustav Rohr, who also worked on Mercedes-Benz's Grand Prix racecars.

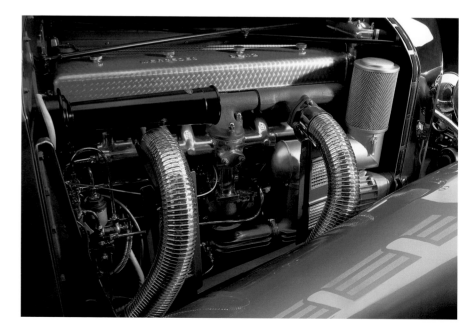

Coachwork on the 540K ranged from quasi-baroque limousines and cabriolets, three Autobahn-Kuriers, and four rather svelte hardtop coupes to elegant roadsters. Noted German *Karosserien* like Erdmann & Rossi in Berlin, as well as stylish French firms like Jacques Saoutchik in Paris, competed for wealthy client commissions. Designed by Hermann Ahrens and built to order by Karosserie Sindelfingen (a Mercedes-Benz in-house coachbuilding subsidiary), the flamboyant 540K Special Roadster was considered the *ne plus ultra* of body styles on this chassis. With its towering V grille, sweeping scallop-edged fenders, arrogantly long hood, tight cabin, low windscreen, and flowing tapered tail, the opulent Special Roadster was expensive and built only to special order. While about four hundred 540Ks were produced, only twenty-six Special Roadsters were completed before the war halted production.

Today, the 540K Special Roadster is considered the pinnacle of German prewar automotive design. As the Mercedes-Benz flagship model of the period, it was virtually hand-built and the quality of its construction was exceptional. Details like its mother-of-pearl instrument panel, rich leather seating, and

twin spotlights flanking a swept-back windshield project a message of speed, power, and exclusivity. Enclosed 540Ks could reach cruising speeds of 100 mph on Germany's then-new autobahns; the lighter Special Roadster was capable of 115 mph. Due to this car's weight (about 5,500 pounds), seventeen-foot length, and advanced suspension, the ride was relatively smooth, but the handling was ponderous and decidedly not sports car–like. Special Roadster owners included Jack Warner, head of Warner Brothers Studios, India's Sultan of Johore, and Nazi leader Hermann Goering. Examples have sold in recent years for more than $8 million, and survivors remain highly prized.

This Special Roadster was a graduation gift to nineteen-year-old Baron Henning Von Krieger from his mother. His sister Gisela was given a 540K Sports Saloon. The Von Krieger family fled to Paris when World War II began, then after Paris fell they went on to London, where the young Baroness was named one of the "10 Most Beautiful Women in the World." After the war, the registration for the Special Roadster was transferred from her brother (who preferred his BMW 328 Cabriolet) to Baroness Gisela, who then immigrated to America, taking the roadster with her on the Queen Mary. The Baroness settled in Manhattan, but summered at the Homestead Inn in Greenwich, Connecticut. The Special Roadster was sequestered in storage at the Homestead, and the Baroness dutifully paid the storage fees for many years after she returned to Europe.

By the mid-1970s, the Mercedes-Benz had become quite valuable, and many people tried to purchase it. George Maley, and occasionally his wife and daughters, made seven trips to Switzerland over twenty years in an effort to buy the car. Although the visits were friendly, the aging Baroness Von Krieger always insisted the car was not for sale. Finally, after living alone for years in squalid circumstances (despite still owning a collection of precious jewelry), the Baroness passed away in 1989.

Dr. James Smith, the owner of the Homestead Inn, claimed ownership of the precious Von Krieger 540K as payment for years of unpaid storage fees. After extended trans-Atlantic litigation, the car was awarded to the Von Krieger heirs. Horst Lautenschlager then bought it from the estate and planned to restore it. The present owners, Lee and Joan Herrington, were able to purchase

Baroness Gisela von Krieger was the owner of this 540K Special Roadster.

the Special Roadster after challenging negotiations, and they arranged for its restoration by Chris Charlton in Oxford, Maine. Lee Herrington observed that the car "was in remarkable, entirely original condition, although the original black paint was peeling off in patches. In the ashtray," he noted, "we found cigarette butts with Gisela's lipstick still on them, and one of her white gloves was under the front seat." One of the best-documented 540K Special Roadsters extant, now beautifully restored, this elegant car won the Pre-war Mercedes-Benz Class at the 2004 Pebble Beach Concours d'Elegance. The car is lent by Lee and Joan Herrington of Bow, New Hampshire.

1938
Alfa Romeo 8C2900B Touring Berlinetta

CHASSIS NO. 412035

Arguably the most sophisticated and technically advanced sports car of its era, the Alfa Romeo 8C2900B rivaled even Bugatti with its elegant blend of advanced styling and engineering. Two very talented men were responsible for the car's creation. Engineer Vittorio Jano had earlier designed Alfa Romeo's successful P-Series Grand Prix racers, as well as its roadgoing sporting models. The body stylist was Felice Bianchi Anderloni, the founder of the coachbuilding firm Carrozzeria Touring in Milan and an early practitioner of lightweight body construction and streamlining.

Jano's competition-proven engine, refined and enlarged for the straight-8-cylinder sports car, offered nearly three liters of displacement, twin overhead camshafts, dual twin-stage superchargers, and a matched pair of updraft Weber carburetors. It developed a then-impressive 180 bhp and could be tuned for 220 bhp or more. Jano, who later worked for Ferrari, keenly understood suspension dynamics and weight distribution; the 8C's handling was enhanced by fully independent front and rear suspension and a four-speed rear transaxle. In an era in which many cars still used cable brakes, the 8C2900B had large hydraulic drums. This model was available in both short- (*Corto*) and long-wheelbase (*Lungo*) configurations. About forty cars in total were made.

Most competitors used relatively heavy frames and body structure to increase chassis stiffness. Rigid axles, favored by many, gave a bone-jarring ride. Along with his chief designer Aquino Gilardi, Anderloni, who had earlier been at the forefront of Italian metallurgical experimentation at Isotta-Fraschini, helped pioneer *Superleggera* (super light) body construction. The technique employed an intricate latticework of small-diameter, lightweight, and very strong steel tubes that, when meticulously welded together on a jig, formed a framework for a beautifully shaped, hand-fashioned aluminum body shell attached to the tubular framing at as few points as possible, with felt pads separating the skin panels and chassis flexions. This process saved a significant amount of weight.

Anderloni's artfully styled Alfa Romeo 8C2900B roadsters and coupes incorporated all that was known about streamlining at the time. The shapes were actually tested on the road. Felt strips were attached to the body and the

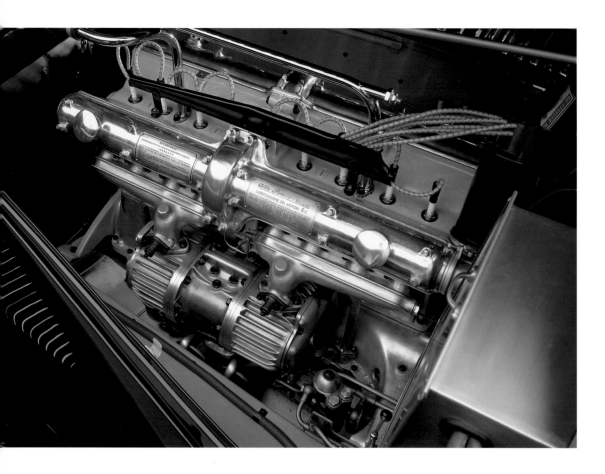

car was then photographed to record how wind flowed over and around the body panels. Anderloni's slender hoods, narrow cockpits and cabins, flowing fender lines, and extended tails were exquisitely proportioned and aerodynamically efficient. On roadsters, a dipped beltline attracted the eye and lent an illusion of movement. The Berlinetta had a slender profile, sharply raked windscreen, fastback roof, and teardrop-shaped rear fenders with slotted skirts, making it both advanced for its era and functional.

By way of proof, 8C2900 Alfas won the grueling 1,000-mile Mille Miglia four times, both before and just after World War II, and they were victorious twice in the 24 Hours of Spa. Alfa Romeo built just thirty 8C2900s, on two wheelbases. This example, chassis number 412035, was first registered in Milan to Società Anonima Montecatini, a forerunner of the present Montedison conglomerate.

This long-wheelbase car's most unusual features include bonnet-side louvers that extend into the cowl scuttle, extended front wings (fenders), and

distinctive rear spats (fender skirts), making it easy to recognize 412035 in Alfa Romeo advertisements in *L'Auto Italiana* and *Moto Aero Cicli e Sports*. The car was owned by the Montecatini company until 1946, when it was sold to Richard Eberhard, then to several other owners. It was later imported into the United States by Frank Griswold, the Pennsylvania-based Alfa Romeo importer. Despite its being a prewar model, Griswold entered 412035 in the first Watkins Glen Grand Prix in 1948 and won. The Berlinetta was subsequently sold and passed through several owners.

In late 1968, Ferrari historian Stan Nowack was working for the Vintage Car Store in Nyack, New York, when he demonstrated the car for former Grand Prix driver Phil Hill (who did not like to drive other people's cars but was interested in purchasing 412035). Nowack told historian Simon Moore about his experience with the 8C2900. "What a delight," Nowack exclaimed. "I had driven a great many pre-war machines, including Bugattis, Bentleys, Duesenbergs, Mercedes-Benz, and others, but none felt as modern as this

Frank Griswold driving his Alfa Romeo to victory in the first Watkins Glen Grand Prix in 1948.

8C2900 Alfa! The steering was light and dead accurate," Nowack continued, "The entire feel of the car denied its pre-war heritage. And it felt like a much smaller car." Nowack concluded, "Certainly it was the best-handling of all the pre-war cars I have driven."

Purchased next by Dr. Donald Vesley of Oklahoma and later Florida, this 8C2900B Berlinetta was unchanged for ten years, then sold to David Cohen, who shipped it to Johannesburg, South Africa. After Cohen realized the car could not be properly restored there, the coupe was transported to the United Kingdom, where it was purchased and impeccably restored by its present owners, Jon and Mary Shirley. Among its many recent triumphs, 412035 won Best of Show honors at the 2008 Pebble Beach Concours d'Elegance, the 2008 Kirkland Island Concours, and the 2009 Villa d'Este Concorso at Lake Como, Italy.

The Alfa Romeo 8C2900B remains one of the fastest, most technically advanced, and most beautiful of all prewar sports cars. We can only imagine what might have followed, had this model's development not been interrupted by a world war. This car is lent by Jon and Mary Shirley of Bellevue, Washington.

1938–1939
Porsche Type 64 (body shell)

REPLICA CHASSIS 38/42

This sleek, streamlined little coupe is Porsche's oldest "ancestor" car, the first in a long line of quick, competent sports and racing models spanning seventy years of development. Ferdinand Porsche, founder of the Porsche dynasty, who had earlier worked at Lohner, Austro-Daimler, and Mercedes-Benz, opened his own design consulting office in 1929 in Stuttgart, Germany. A brilliant engineer and theoretician, he subsequently worked for Steyr, and later for Auto-Union, where he designed that firm's legendary rear-engine Grand Prix cars. Porsche also designed the original Volkswagen Kdf-Wagen, the model that made his name famous throughout the world.

Porsche and his talented staff, including his son Ferdinand (known as Ferry), worked on several Volkswagen Kdf-Wagen variations, including the right-hand-drive Type 66, a Type 67 ambulance, and an open-sided cross-country model called the Type 62, which later morphed into the Type 82, a Jeep-like Kubelwagen. In 1937 Porsche began work on a sports-car version of the VW called the Type 64. The initial plans for the Type 64 proposed enlarging the 1.0-liter VW flat-4 engine to 1.5 liters, adding an aluminum body and raising the top speed potential to 95 mph. As his firm became more successful, Porsche espoused the idea of building his own sports car and assigned a team to work on what was to be called the Type 114, also known as the F-Wagen. The mechanical drawings were never completed, but by January of 1939 the car had been fully conceptualized, and many drawings still exist. Resembling the chassis of the Auto-Union Grand Prix racer, the engine was to be located between the passengers and the rear axle, with the transmission placed behind the axle. Changing his mind, Porsche planned a then-radical 1.5-liter V-10 power plant, anticipating the V-10 Formula 1 engines of the present. Erwin Komenda styled the curvaceous and startlingly modern body, which resembled a stretched and aerodynamic Volkswagen coupe. Porsche planned to produce this new car as soon as world tensions subsided.

Germany felt it needed its own new long-distance auto competition. The Italians had the 1,000-mile Mille Miglia road race, but it had been canceled in 1939 because of a horrific accident the year before. Spearheaded by the National Socialist Motoring Corps (NSKK), plans were developed for a Berlin-to-Rome,

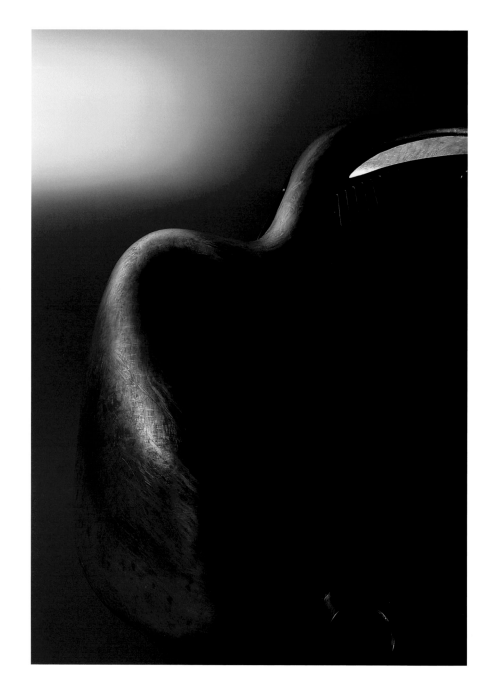

1,500-kilometer (900-mile) long-distance race. The major German automakers, along with Alfa Romeo, were going to create special streamlined cars for this high-speed event. Work began despite the start of war, since many Italians and Germans believed the European conflict would last only a few months.

Porsche and his colleagues viewed the long-distance race announcement as a public relations opportunity. They convinced the National Sporting Authority (ONS) to commission three sports coupes based on the Volkswagen Type 60, to be called Type 60K10, and the cars were also known as the VW Aerocoupes. These cars would use the VW platform frame, a highly tuned Volkswagen engine with dual carburetors developing about 50 bhp, and a streamlined, fully-enclosed body built by Reutter Coachworks in Stuttgart. The design—again by Komenda and tested in a wind tunnel—retained the VW oval rear window, window patterns, and hood louvers. The decklid covering

the engine opened sideways. It also had full skirts on all four fenders and a very low cabin that resembled a single-seater. The driver and passenger seats were staggered so there would be sufficient room for the two occupants. Twin spare tires were located under the hood, as was a large fuel tank. The new car, weighing just 1,870 pounds and capable of more than 95 mph, was ready, but the ill-timed Berlin–Rome road race was canceled.

The three Type 60K10 / Type 64 Aerocoupes were subsequently fitted with horns and flip-out trafficators (turn signals) and then driven on the road. Bodo Laferenz, a senior VW deputy, damaged one of the cars in a collision; Ferdinand Porsche and his chauffeur Josef Goldinger used the other two. Reportedly, the two men drove from Fallersleben, near Wolfsburg, to the Hotel Bristol in the center of Berlin, averaging a remarkable 85 mph door-to-door. Only one of these cars, owned by the Porsche family, survived the war.

Porsche Type 64 on the road, ca. 1939.

Porsche Type 64 in the yard of the Porsche villa in Stuttgart, Germany, ca. 1939.

The trendsetting Porsche Type 64 Berlin–Rome racecar is widely regarded by historians as the ancestor of all subsequent Porsche sports models. Ahead of its time, its frame, engine location, suspension layout, aerodynamics, and general body shape anticipated all the postwar Porsches. In conjunction with the opening of the new Porsche Museum in Stuttgart, Germany, Porsche commissioned an exact model of the Type 64 body shell. A re-creation of the first car to display the Porsche name, this replica was handcrafted by metal wizard Hubert Drescher in Hinterzarden, Germany. The chassis number 38/42 was stamped with vintage tools. The 163.3-inch-long body was accurately replicated using painstaking measurements taken from dozens of historic black-and-white photographs, some of which were shot in front of the old Porsche works building in Stuttgart-Zuffenhausen. Jurgen Zeyer, writing in the Porsche magazine *Christophorus*, reports that Drescher ran his fingers over the old photographs "so as to be able to understand the old forms and the lines, and thus to gain a sense of the proportions of such things as the transition between the covered wheelwells and the hood. One thing he noticed," Zeyer points out, "was the slight convexity of the door, designed in this way to increase its stiffness. 'We tried to place ourselves in the mindset of that time,' Drescher said."

Its aluminum alloy gleaming, the Porsche Type 64 shell is a mute testimonial to the brilliance of Ferdinand Porsche and his colleagues. Its advanced and elegant shape speaks volumes about how Porsche has always trod its own path in automobile design and engineering, and it still does. This replica is lent by Porsche AG, Stuttgart, Germany, and Porsche Cars North America.

1939
Talbot-Lago T-150-C-SS

CHASSIS NO. 51620

The sporting Talbot-Lago T-150-C chassis inspired open roadsters and closed cars, most notably a series of curvaceous custom coupes. These cars were sensational in their heyday, and remain highly valued today. Streamlined, sleek, and light enough to race competitively, they were called *Goutte d'Eau* (drop of water) and in English they quickly became known as the "Teardrop" Talbots. Famed Parisian carrossiers Joseph Figoni and Ovidio Falaschi built twelve "New York-style" Talbot-Lago coupes between 1937 and 1939, so-called because the first was introduced at the New York Auto Show. Five more were built in a different notchback Teardrop style and were named "Jeancart," after a wealthy French patron who commissioned the first example. Historian Richard Adatto, who wrote the definitive work on French streamlined styling noted that it took the Figoni and Falaschi craftsmen some 2,100 hours of painstaking work to complete a custom body. No two Teardrop coupes were exactly alike.

To the delight of sportsmen and select coachbuilders, Talbot's president, Antony Lago, later offered a top-of-the-line SS (Super Sport) version on the T-150-C's sturdy ladder frame, with independent wishbones in front and a live rear axle. The competition engine, a lusty 4-liter six topped with a hemispherical combustion chamber head, could be fitted with three carburetors for more than 170 bhp. Its innovative Wilson pre-selector gearbox was produced by a firm that was coincidentally owned by Lago. Gear selection was effected by a fingertip-actuated lever that permitted instant shifts, without the driver having to take his hand off the steering wheel. These cars were quick and reliable: in 1938, a competition-prepared T-150-C-SS Coupe finished third at the 24 Hours of Le Mans.

Carrosserie Pourtout in Paris rivaled Figoni and Falaschi in the production of lovely, aerodynamic art-deco coachwork on Delahaye, Delage, Talbot-Lago, Bugatti, Hispano-Suiza, and other classic French chassis. Richard Adatto stated definitively: "Marcel Pourtout was a master coachbuilder." Working with his partners Emile Darl'mat, a Paris fine car dealer, and Georges Paulin, a brilliant designer, Pourtout catered to an upmarket clientele that included French prime minister Georges Clemenceau and Greek banker and fine car fancier André Embiricos.

This elegant berlinetta was built by Marcel Pourtout's coachbuilding firm. It was styled by his top designer, Georges Paulin, who had earlier sketched a one-of-a-kind Bentley coupe for André Embiricos. A perfectly proportioned fastback, it represents yet another exquisite variation on the dramatic teardrop style. More masculine and arguably more aggressive in looks than the earlier Figoni efforts (and one of just four examples built), it was commissioned by Monsieur Parent, a wealthy amateur racer. He competed in a few regional events, but did not run the coupe at the 24 Hour Race at Le Mans, as that event was cancelled from 1940 to 1946, due to the hostilities in Europe.

Georges Paulin was initially trained as a dental technician, but he loved fine automobiles. Persistent and fortunate, he was eventually able to set aside his dental practice and work full-time as a custom body designer. His tri-umphs included a remarkable folding metal top for Peugeot, which started his automotive career and earned him a great deal of attention. Paulin designed the art-deco, delightfully petite Peugeot Darl'mat 302 sports roadster and the incomparable Embiricos Bentley as well as a fully custom Delage D8-120 coupe of unparalleled proportions, and this series of four teardrop variation coupes for Pourtout, to name just a few of his accomplishments.

Unlike the arguably more voluptuous Figoni & Falaschi teardrop designs, where there is nary a straight line to be found, this fine Paulin/Pourtout collaboration is both angular and swoopy at the same time. With a more upright grille and covered headlamps leading the way, its long hood flows quickly rearward into the slanted and split windscreen, then the lines extend in a continuous radius all the way back to a gracefully tapered tail. Large bumpers

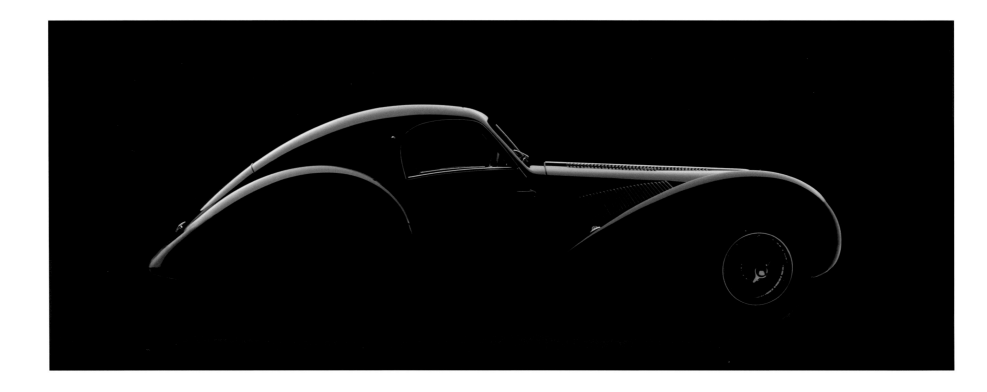

would only clutter this design, although sister cars 90121 and 90122 sport thin protective appendages that hardly detract from each car's appearance. This car may have been fitted with similar units, but they are long gone. Its fully skirted rear fenders and rakish window line are reminiscent of the legendary Bugatti Type 57SC Atlantic, but this is a unique effort—luckily, all four examples have survived.

Offered a top position at Rolls-Royce in England, although he spoke no English, Paulin designed the elegant, art-moderne, and pioneering Rolls-Royce Corniche, a forerunner to the firm's postwar cars. When the war began, the patriotic Paulin returned to France, and despite ill health he bravely joined the French Resistance. He became a principal in the clandestine spy network known as "Alibi." His specialty was making precise drawings of German military installations and armaments. As a result of a notorious act of cowardice, Paulin was betrayed, along with several of his colleagues, by a French double

agent. Georges Paulin was tried and executed by Nazi soldiers in March 1942; it was a terrible waste of an extraordinary talent.

Stored safely away in a warehouse in Marseille, No. 90119 was raced after the war by Domenic Sales. An American, David Leopold, saw the car in Paris, and shipped it home. The Talbot-Lago passed through a succession of owners and was offered to the early French car collector Vojta Mashek for $3,250 cash (or a '54 or '55 Porsche plus $750). Mashek, who owned and raced a similar example, chassis No. 90121, declined to buy this car, and the lovely coupe subsequently went through four more owners: John Norsym, Hal Raitt, Earl Brown, and Stuart Bewly, who bought 90119 in 1988, won a Third Place award with it at the Pebble Beach Concours d'Elegance in 1991, then sold it to the present owner in 2000. At Meadow Brook Hall in 2001, it won the coveted David R. Holls Designer's Choice Trophy. This Talbot-Lago was lent by Deborah and Arturo Keller of the Pyramid Collection, Petaluma, California.

1948
Tucker Model 48 Torpedo

NO. 1034

Preston Tucker of Ypsilanti, Michigan, initially gained fame when he promoted an ill-fated racing effort for the 1935 Indianapolis 500, pairing the unlikely duo of Henry Miller and Henry Ford to build innovative front-drive, flathead Ford-powered two-man racers. None of the cars finished, mainly due to a repeated malfunction that resulted because each car's left-side exhaust header was located too close to its steering box, heating the lubricant and causing the steering unit to seize. But Tucker had his successes. His electrically powered gun turret proved to be a profitable venture during World War II. When the war ended, he was thinking even bigger.

Tucker's plan for a radical postwar car first appeared in the December 1946 issue of *Science Illustrated* magazine. His efforts defied convention with an unusual design—a full-size sedan powered by a rear-mounted, air-cooled 589 cid flat-6. The giant engine would provide fast acceleration, but it would be barely idling at 60 mph, while yielding excellent 24-mile-per-gallon fuel economy. For his futuristic "dream car," Tucker considered then-unproven Kinmont "Safe-Stop" disc brakes, and insisted on a four-speed preselector gearbox.

The realities of timing, availability, and cost led to the production of Tucker's horizontally opposed, 334-cid OHV (overhead valve) six. Based on an aluminum Franklin/Aircooled Motors helicopter engine, it was converted to water cooling for the Tucker. The plans for disc brakes were dropped as they were too expensive. After rebuilding a few secondhand Cord 810/812 gearboxes, Tucker developed its own four-speed based on the Cord design, with a Bendix vacuum-electric preselector. The Tucker's "Torsiolastic" suspension featured independent front A-arms and rear trailing links, all hinged in rubber. The engine could be removed in a matter of minutes for easy servicing.

In an era when most production sedans had just 100 to 125 bhp, the Tucker's lazy 166 bhp at 3,200 rpm (probably a conservative rating) and whopping 372 pounds/feet of torque, meant that the 4,235-pound Model 48 was easily the fastest American car of its time. Legendary writer Ken W. Purdy claims to have driven a Tucker at more than 125 mph. The Marquis de Portago, a famous Grand Prix driver, reportedly topped 131 mph in a Tucker test

Assembly line producing the Tucker flat-6, adapted from a helicopter engine, 1948.

at Sebring. *Mechanix Illustrated*'s pioneer road tester Tom McCahill raved about the Tucker's ten-second 0-to-60 time and called it one of "the greatest performing automobiles ever built on this side of the Atlantic." (A 1948 Cadillac, with its 150 bhp flathead V-8, took more than thirteen seconds to accelerate from 0 to 60 and reached 100 mph top speed.) Tucker's prodigious torque rating wouldn't be topped for years. With its rocket-ship styling by Alex Tremulis, rear-mounted engine, aircraft-style doors, pop-out windshield, swiveling center headlight, standard seat belts, and padded "safety chamber," there was nothing like it on the road. Orders poured in for the "Car of Tomorrow." Tucker's $2,450 price tag undercut Cadillac's popular Model 62 sedan by about $500—a big difference in 1948.

But Preston Tucker's rear-engine Torpedo never reached full production. Myths abound about the short-lived Tucker venture. People persist in thinking that the major automakers were determined to kill off this competitor and that "a loosely-organized conspiracy between the carmakers, the Securities and Exchange Commission, and the Chicago District Attorney's office brought him down." Tucker was said to be a devious, flamboyant self-promoter who misappropriated funds, spent lavishly, and never intended to build cars. But little of that is true. Preston Tucker was fundamentally naïve about business, his effort was seriously underfunded, his flamboyant style annoyed the powers that be, the hastily built cars were not sufficiently developed, and he was very unlucky. Despite Tucker's business failure, owners and club members remain loyal to his memory. They are happy to expound on what their hero might have done to the arrogant Detroit infrastructure had he not been indicted, his plant closed, and all his records seized. The Tucker Automobile Club of America's motto remains "Keeping the Legend Alive." After Tucker was acquitted of all charges, poor publicity and lack of funds doomed efforts to resume production. Following an ill-fated attempt to build a car called the Carioca in South America, Preston Tucker died of lung cancer in 1956.

With its rear-mounted engine on a long, 130-inch wheelbase and lopsided 42/58 weight distribution, the Tucker feels ponderous. Its steering is vague and sloppy, and it oversteers at the slightest provocation. But under

hard acceleration, the six flashy chrome exhaust extensions blat like a big Chris-Craft runabout, the nose lifts, and the Tucker accelerates very quickly.

The Tucker pictured here, No. 1034, a Model 48 Torpedo sedan in "Waltz Blue," was lent by the Cofer Collection of Tucker, Georgia, to the exhibition at the High Museum of Art. The nearly identical example on display at the Portland Art Museum is Tucker No. 1007, initially purchased from the factory by a Midwest dealer as a demonstrator. Nothing is known about its history until 1985, when it was acquired by a Japanese businessman. No. 1007 was shipped to Japan and remained there until the 1990s, when its owner was involved in a bankruptcy. As part of the settlement, the Tucker was sold to a Texas oilman from the Dallas-Ft. Worth area. When his business failed, the Tucker was sold at a Barrett-Jackson auction to Robert E. and Margie Petersen, founders of the Petersen Automotive Museum in Los Angeles. In 2002 Tucker No. 1007

passed to its present owners. Originally green, now painted "Waltz Blue," it has been restored to its original condition except for its wheel covers. On this early example, when high beams are selected and the steering wheel is turned more than ten degrees, the centrally mounted "Cyclops" headlamp rotates with the front wheels. From Tucker No. 1026 onward, the center light's mechanical linkage was replaced with a more effective cable. Tucker No. 1007 is lent by The LeMay Family Collection, compliments of LeMay—America's Car Museum, Tacoma, Washington.

1953
Porsche 550

PROTOTYPE, SERIAL NO. 550-01

Porsche's unprecedented success as a sports and racing car manufacturer began with this car, the first of two 550 prototypes, and the firm's initial purpose-built Porsche racing car. Founder Dr. Ing. Ferdinand Porsche led a successful design consultancy in Stuttgart, Germany, before World War II. He had previously worked at Austro-Daimler, designed and developed racing cars at Auto-Union, and designed the first Volkswagen. When the war ended in 1945, surviving Porsche employees were working in Gmünd, Austria, renovating farm implements and cars. Porsche himself and members of his team were invited to consult on the design of the Renault 4CV sedan, soon to be a Volkswagen rival. While in France, Porsche was interned for two years on false charges relating to a wartime plant he had managed. He was ransomed with funds earned from his design of a radical mid-engine Grand Prix racer for Piero Dusio and Cisitalia.

In 1948 Porsche's son Ferdinand "Ferry" Porsche built a Volkswagen-based "special" roadster that received acclaim after a Swiss magazine had published

a favorable road test. The first Porsche production car—a coupe designed by Porsche's body engineer/designer Erwin Komenda and built in a small series—was known as the 356, because it was Job 356 in the design studio's production. Sleek, streamlined, lightweight, and innovative, the little two-seater used a strong platform frame and a modified VW 1,131 cc, horizontally opposed, air-cooled four-cylinder engine, mounted behind the rear axle. Its suspension was independent all around with torsion bars, front trailing links, and rear swing axles. Despite its primitive cable brakes and being limited to an 85 mph top speed, it handled extremely well. 356s were soon being successfully raced by a growing cadre of enthusiastic owners.

The Porsche Design Studios returned to Germany in 1950. Car production increased, with the bodies initially being made by Reutter. Porsche's financial success (the one-thousandth car was sold in 1951) was supplemented by a royalty received on each Volkswagen built and from licensing a Porsche transmission synchromesh system initially developed for the Cisitalia GP racecar.

Porsche also owned Allgaier, a company that built a range of diesel-powered farm tractors. The elder Porsche died early in 1951, but not before he saw his cars beginning to challenge the world's best.

Ferry Porsche understood that without large advertising budgets, racing was the way to prove Porsche's superiority and capture world attention. With its displacement reduced to 1,086 cc, a single Porsche qualified for the 1,100 cc Class at the 24 Hours of Le Mans in 1951, won in its first appearance there, and finished twentieth overall. Enthusiastic American servicemen brought a few Porsches home from Germany. On these shores, imported by Max Hoffman, an Austrian friend of the Porsche family and a distributor of imports in the United States, the low, streamlined little cars attracted a great deal of interest. And Porsche would repeat its Le Mans class-winning feat in 1952.

But Ferry Porsche realized that modified production cars alone would not be able to win major races. Earlier, modified privateer Gmünd coupes—a small series of fifty alloy-bodied cars built by Porsche in Austria—and the Glöckler-Porsche racecars (built by Frankfurt VW distributor Walter Glöckler and his workshop chief Hermann Ramelow) proved Porsche design principles could be very competitive in small-displacement classes. Accordingly, Porsche designed its own purpose-built racecar specifically for competition.

Project 550, a racing coupe designed for the lowest possible aerodynamic drag, was introduced in 1952. Its pushrod 1,498 cc production-car engine benefited from larger twin-choke Solex carburetors and other modifications that reportedly increased its power to 98 bhp on alcohol fuel. An external oil cooler, mounted in the nose, was paired with a wet-sump lubrication system. A new transmission using Porsche synchromesh, and a limited-slip differential were part of the specification. Like Glöckler, Porsche contracted Weidenhausen of Frankfurt to build the light alloy bodies and removable hardtops for the two cars being readied for the 1953 season. The first completed 550 actually competed as a roadster in its initial race at the Nürburgring, driven by Helmut "Helm" Glöckler (Walter Glöckler's cousin). He would doubtless have preferred for the 550 to have had its hardtop installed (it rained heavily), but he bested rival competitors Borgward and Eisenacher Motorenwerk (EMW), overcame carburetion problems, and won the race, adding the Porsche 550 to that short list of racecars that were victorious in their first competitive effort.

A Porsche 550 coupe won its class at Le Mans in 1953. Its sister car finished second.

At Le Mans that year, veteran driver Hans Hermann joined Helm Glöckler in 550-01, and a pair of driver-journalists, Richard von Frankenberg and Paul Frère, drove 550-02. During practice, with the coupe tops fitted, the two Porsches reached 124 mph on the Mulsanne Straight. But the cars lacked ventilation, the low tops were claustrophobic, and the noise levels were intense due to a lack of soundproofing. Still, the two Porsche coupes ran consistently within a lap of each other for the entire twenty-four hours and crossed the finish line at the same interval at which they started. Le Mans scorers abhorred a tie, so the class win was awarded to 550-02. The racing journalists had won the 1,500 cc class and set a new record.

At the season's end, both cars were shipped to the Automobile Club of Guatemala and a group of Porsche enthusiasts headed by Jaroslav Juhan, who raced them in La Carrera Panamericana in Mexico (550-02 took its class, co-driven by Jose Herrate) and the 1,000-kilometer race in Buenos Aires (550-01 won, driven by Juhan and Asturias Hall), as well as at Sebring (550-01 finished tenth overall) and in many other races. Accolades poured in: "These incredible Porsches," *Autosport* wrote. "Potent Porsches" was the headline in Britain's *Autocar*. Successful on three continents, the 550's initial successes showed Porsche was serious about racing.

For years, Porsche enthusiasts believed the two 550 prototypes had vanished. It was true for 550-02, but 550-01 survived in a warehouse in Mexico. Its original aluminum shell was worn from years of competition, so Salvador Lopes-Chavez, who had finished fifth in the car in the 1954 La Carrera Panamericana, had a fiberglass body molded using the aluminum panels as a buck. Although Miles Collier had known about 550-01 for years, the car was not for sale. When it finally became available, Joe Cavaglieri Restoration of Sherman Oaks, California, painstakingly handcrafted a new aluminum body. Assistance during the ground-up restoration came from Alfredo Leal, the mechanic for 550-01 during the 1954 La Carrera Panamericana. After five years of work, the impeccably restored 550-01 was the Concours de Sport Best of Show winner at Amelia Island in 2005. This car is lent by Miles Collier and the Collier Collection, Naples, Florida.

1954
Dodge Firearrow III

NO. 1034

Encouraged by the success of General Motors' lavish traveling Motoramas and driven by the postwar public's enthusiasm for so-called concept cars or "dream cars," Virgil M. Exner, head of Chrysler Styling and responsible for remaking Chrysler's rather stodgy late-1940s image, turned to Carrozzeria Ghia in Turin, Italy, to produce a series of one-of-a-kind "idea cars" on production Chrysler, Dodge, and Plymouth chassis. Exner himself had designed the acclaimed Chrysler K-310 series, which was followed by three more Ghia-built Chrysler design studies: the C-200, the SS, and the D'Elegance, as well as the De Soto Adventurer coupe. While these creations were met with approval, none were slated for production. For his next venture, Exner tapped Luigi Segre of Ghia to produce a memorable quartet of cars for Dodge called the Firearrows.

The first Dodge Firearrow, a lowslung, open two-seater, was introduced at the 1953 Turin Auto Show. With its dual headlights, a dramatic oval grille bisected with a propeller-like center bar, a chrome "belly band" that bisected the body and ran completely around it, and a low, frameless windshield, the Firearrow I was a big hit when shown at Chrysler's New York showrooms. Built for display only, this concept car had no engine. Despite a premature announcement that a hundred examples would be made, the lovely Firearrow I was never scheduled for even limited production. *Motor Trend's* Bob D'Olivo called it "perhaps the most successful meeting of European and U.S. designs." A second Ghia styling exercise followed. The Firearrow II, built on a 119-inch Dodge wheelbase, repeated its predecessor's large grille but without the large horizontal grille bar; there were only two headlights, molded higher in the fenders, and the trademark four chromed exhaust pipes were carried over. A 6½-foot-wide cockpit could seat three abreast. The Firearrow II rode on chromed wire wheels and was powered by a 241 cid Dodge Hemi V-8 developing 150 bhp.

Soon afterward, Ghia produced the Dodge Firearrow III, a stunning, low-roofed sports coupe, finished in metallic opal blue, that presented yet another variation on the previous cars' oversized grille treatment—this time with vertical concave teeth. Quad headlights (two of which were high-intensity driving

lights), a smartly raked windshield, a wraparound rear window, abbreviated bumpers, and a painted belly band helped distinguish this latest Italian exotic from its show-car predecessors. The four chrome exhaust pipes, mounted two each in the rear fenders, were fully functional, as were the large side scoops, resembling those on Ferraris and Maseratis, positioned to help cool the engine compartment.

Inside the Firearrow III's snug cockpit, which was finished in luscious opal blue and white pleated leather, two oversized instrument dials flanked the steering column, which was topped with an elegant three-spoke, wood-rimmed Nardi steering wheel. A slender lever operated the Power-Flite automatic transmission. The Firearrow III's large decklid, with its subtly peaked center ridge, was operated by a push-button. Two small, round tail lights, mounted under twin reflectors, were faired into the trailing edges of the discreet rear

fins. The wheel openings were not fully round, but were flat on top, so as not to interrupt the sweep of the sidetrim. The wheels were chromed wires with simulated twin-ear knockoff hubs. Whitewall tires underscored the notion that this was more a boulevard sports cruiser than a hard-edged GT car—an athletic American wearing a stylish Italian fitted suit.

Mounted on the 119-inch-wheelbase Dodge chassis, the Firearrow was powered by a 150 bhp, 241 cid Dodge "Red Ram" Hemi V-8, but some sources claim the engine was at one point modified for more horsepower when popular aviatrix Betty Skelton, who had set NASCAR speed records at Daytona Beach, lapped the newly dedicated Chrysler Proving Grounds track in June 1954 at a closed-course record-setting pace of 143.44 mph, while wearing a dress and high heels (see page 97). In its coverage of the event, *Motor Trend* quipped, "Who says show cars don't run and women can't have a lead foot?"

Betty Skelton at the Chrysler Proving Grounds in Chelsea, Michigan, 1954.

The Firearrow III would prove to be a precursor for the De Soto Adventurer II and Plymouth Explorer concept vehicles that quickly followed. A Firearrow IV was also built—basically a convertible version of the Firearrow III, but with four seats. The rear seats were removable to create a cargo area.

After the Firearrow III had starred on the U.S. auto show circuit, Chrysler was obliged to ship the car back to Italy to avoid paying large duties on it. It was sold to a private owner in France, where it would remain for the next thirty years. In the 1980s, Dave Holls, then General Motors Chief of Design, saw a letter to a magazine editor from the owner of the Firearrow III, looking for information on the car. He alerted a prominent American collector that the car was still in existence. After some negotiation, the Firearrow III was purchased, brought to the United States, and fully restored by Fran Roxas. Sold to

its present owner at the RM Automobiles of Arizona Auction in January 2009, the Firearrow III is the only concept car that ever set a speed record. Many of its design elements influenced Chrysler styling for years to come, as well as the limited-production, four-passenger Dual-Ghia automobiles (just 117 were made) favored by Frank Sinatra, Dean Martin, Sammy Davis, Jr., and other members of the "Rat Pack." By virtue of their influence on Chrysler's production models, the four Dodge Firearrows were immensely effective in helping to rejuvenate the company's image. Under Virgil Exner, and with assistance from Ghia, Chrysler's acclaimed "Forward Look" styling of 1955–1961 sent General Motors and Ford designers scurrying back to their drawing boards to revise designs that simply could not match Chrysler's fresh, Italian-inspired flair. The car is lent by David J. Disiere of Irving, Texas.

1955
Mercedes-Benz 300SLR "Uhlenhaut" Coupe

Less than a decade after World War II ended, Mercedes-Benz—having survived the virtual destruction of its factories—was intently competing for the World Sports Car Championship with its radical W196S roadster, known as the 300SLR. Based on the successful W196 Formula 1 Grand Prix racer, the SLR (*Sport, Leicht, Rennen*, or Sport, Light, Racing) was a sleek, highly-advanced, front-mid-engine design with a dual-overhead-camshaft straight-8 engine mounted behind the front suspension for optimal front/rear weight distribution. Thanks to a strong but lightweight space-frame chassis and minimalist Elektron magnesium alloy bodywork, the SLR weighed just 1,936 pounds.

The 300SLR's advanced 3.0-liter I-8 aluminum alloy engine featured fuel injection and then-novel desmodromic valves that opened and closed mechanically, permitting a high red-line of 8,500 rpm. The engine protruded right into the cockpit, so agile drivers had to straddle the driveshaft and the bell housing to reach the brake and clutch pedals. A straight-8's long crankshaft flexed, so the geared power takeoff from the engine was located in the center of the

block. The dry-sump engine could be tuned to develop up to 310 bhp. It was canted 33 degrees for a low silhouette, and it rose just above the hoodline so that a distinctive offset hood blister was required.

The brakes were enormous inboard-mounted, finned hydraulic drums that were mechanically linked with connecting shafts. Originally, the rear-drive SLR was designed for four-wheel drive but that never materialized. Independent A-arm front and rear suspension, the latter with a low-roll-center swing axle, ensured adroit handling. The SLR burned a potent high-octane mixture of 65 percent low-lead gasoline and 35 percent benzine laced with alcohol.

In the 1950s, Italy's Mille Miglia (a 1,000-mile road race from Brescia through the mountains to Rome and back to Brescia) was considered a true test of both men and machines. A Mercedes-Benz SLR won convincingly in 1955, averaging nearly 100 mph for ten hours and 1,000 miles, with British driver Stirling Moss and his navigator, Denis Jenkinson. Two years later, in 1957, the Marquis Alfonso de Portago's Ferrari roared off the road,

Rudolf Uhlenhaut with his 300SLR in 1955.

mowing down spectators. A shocked Italian government ended the official Mille Miglia for all time (an historic rally called the Mille Miglia Storica takes place annually). Moss and Jenkinson's remarkable 1955 record was never to be broken.

For the 24 Hours of Le Mans in 1955, to counter the factory Jaguars with their efficient new disc brake system, Mercedes-Benz developed a novel air brake for its SLRs, consisting of a 7½-square-foot aluminum spoiler that could be hydraulically raised and lowered to increase wind resistance and improve braking effectiveness. When SLR driver Pierre Levegh braked hard to avoid a suddenly slowing car, he crashed. The fuel-laden SLR's magnesium body exploded on impact, killing Levegh and more than eighty spectators. Although World Champion Juan Manuel Fangio was leading in a sister SLR, Mercedes withdrew its remaining entries out of consideration for the many dead and injured.

Mercedes-Benz won four additional major sports car races that year, captured the World Sports Car Championship, and then retired from all competition. Racing consumed huge amounts of money and the time of countless engineers. By 1955 Mercedes-Benz was building 50,000 passenger cars annually. They had won both the Formula 1 and sports car crowns. Werner Engle won the European Rally Championship, alternating between a 220S and a 300SL, and Paul O'Shea's 300SL Gullwing had been successful in SCCA races. Having made its point, the company elected to focus on its growing worldwide retail business.

Beginning in 1936, Rudolf Uhlenhaut was in charge of Mercedes-Benz's racing program. Under his guidance, the famed "Silver Arrows" of the 1930s dominated European Grand Prix racing. The son of a German father and a British mother, he was not only a talented engineer, but also an expert racer, who was as consistently fast as the factory drivers. Piloting a W196 Formula 1 Grand Prix car in earnest, Uhlenhaut occasionally surpassed Fangio's times in test sessions, but Mercedes considered him too valuable to permit him to race.

Originally, nine SLRs were created for the sports car competition program. In 1955, before the decision was made to stop competing, Uhlenhaut had two of the roadsters transformed into ultra-light, hyperfast, beautifully aerodynamic coupes. They used a slightly wider version of the roadster chassis, and because of the high door-sill beams the signature gullwing doors were required. While they resembled the production 300SL Gullwings, the SLR coupes shared not a single component with the road-going models. These rare cars were used a few times in team practices, but they never competed in an actual race. Uhlenhaut reportedly drove one, virtually a street-legal competition car, to and from work. Legend has it that once when he was late for an important meeting, he dashed from Munich to Stuttgart, a trip that normally took two-and-one-half hours, in just over one hour. Author Karl Ludvigsen called the SLR coupe "one of the most charismatic Mercedes-Benz cars ever made."

Weighing just 2,176 pounds dry, the twin coupes were a personal project for Uhlenhaut, who drove them to racing events throughout Europe. There was no sound-deadening, so the driver and passenger were obliged to wear earplugs. A large, suitcase-sized external muffler was attached on the right-hand side to quiet the exhaust. The coupes' quick-release steering wheel, outside-laced wire wheels with prominent knock-off hubcaps, large side vents for engine cooling, straight exhausts, lack of bumper protection, and rear-facing vents marked them as true racing cars. An SLR coupe could sprint to 60 mph in 6.8 seconds and was timed by the Swiss magazine *Automobil Revue* at 176.47 mph. Mercedes-Benz considered building a small series (ten to twenty) of these cars, to be priced at $30,000 to $40,000, but nothing came of it.

Today the two cars, owned by Mercedes-Benz, are exercised occasionally and remain a rolling tribute to the genius of Rudolf Uhlenhaut. This car is lent by the Mercedes-Benz Museum, Stuttgart, Germany.

1957
Cadillac Eldorado Brougham

Cadillac refused to be upstaged by Lincoln's elegant 1956 Continental Mark II. General Motors had long been developing its own exclusive top-of-the-line statement. In truth, Cadillac's counter-car was not really a secret. The public had been conditioned to seeing visions for the future at the GM Motoramas, held from 1951 to 1961 in venues across the country. The shows displayed GM's creativity, styling leadership, sheer inventiveness, and optimism. The Motoramas began with "Transportation Unlimited" in 1949, followed by "Mid-Century Motorama" in 1950. Those first exhibitions did not feature what are now called "dream cars" or "concept cars." Beginning in 1951 for the first official GM Motorama, and over the next ten years, more than fifty concept cars (the exact number remains uncertain) were presented in a series of remarkable automotive extravaganzas. GM also featured custom production models, equipped with special paint, upholstery, accessories, and trim.

Created to tease the public, the Motoramas gave show-goers a glimpse of the future, gauged enthusiasm for advanced features, and tested public reaction to dramatic styling cues. The intent was to display design expertise and advanced engineering, while encouraging the purchase of new GM vehicles. These shows flourished, grew in scope and complexity—featuring elaborate turntables and multilevel, cantilevered platforms to display the cars, along with actors, singers, and dancers in musical revues—and then died because the escalating cost of ever-more-elaborate displays ultimately outpaced the sales and public relations benefit.

The Motoramas presented a future with improbable cars like the dazzling Firebird trio, based on aircraft designs, which had little likelihood of production. Today, auto stylists still attempt to push the envelope with eye-catching shapes, but the major premise now is to prepare potential buyers for a dramatic shift in design that can lead to production models and sales successes. That is what happened with the Cadillac Eldorado Brougham.

1957 magazine advertisement

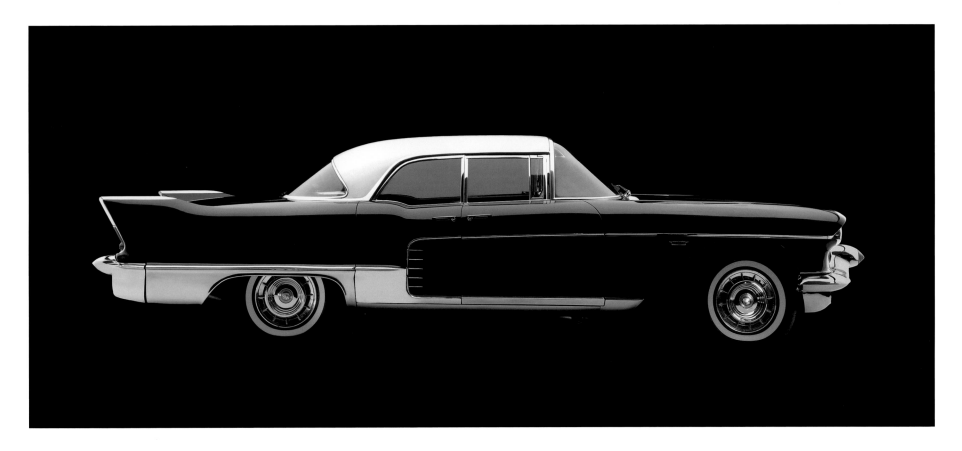

At the 1953 GM Motorama, Cadillac presented the Orleans, a smartly styled, pillarless four-door sedan, with "suicide" rear doors (hinged on the trailing edge). The following year, Cadillac's show cars included the Park Avenue, another four-door hardtop in "Antoinette Blue" that presaged the 1955 production car's styling, and the XP-38, the first Eldorado Brougham prototype, finished in iridescent "Chameleon Green." The lowslung XP-38 featured panoramic (wraparound) front and rear windshields, had a wheel base that had been shortened from 129 to 124 inches, and stood just over 54 inches high.

For 1956, two more Brougham concept cars made their debuts—the XP-48 Town Car and a prototype that was a close precursor to the production Brougham. Working under Harley J. Earl, the founder of GM's pioneering Art & Color Studios, Ed Glowacke was the Brougham's principal designer. When the actual model appeared in 1957, nationwide audiences had seen the prototypes and were already favorably disposed. What shocked many people was the new Series 70 Eldorado Brougham's $13,074 price tag—nearly three times the price of a base Series 62 sedan and a considerable increase from the original estimate of $8,500. For that lofty sum, buyers received America's first four-door pillarless hardtop (even the ventipanes were omitted). At last, decades after the classic era, Cadillac was offering a hand-built luxury car that was designed to compete with the Rolls-Royce Silver Cloud.

The Brougham's egg-crate grille and its quad headlights, available for the first time on any car, were stylish and unique. A long sculpted body cove that ended in an air scoop with five chromed windsplits helped define the Brougham's sides. The hardtop's openness was accentuated by the front-opening rear doors. Other styling touches included ribbed lower rear panels that extended along the rocker sills, discreet shark-fin rear fenders capped with chrome, a rear bumper with miniature "dagmars" (bullet-shaped protrusions named for a buxom TV personality), and—the crowning touch—a very elegant brushed stainless steel hardtop roof. Smaller and trimmer than conventional Cadillac sedans, the Brougham's horizontal chromed accents actually made it appear more slender than its stablemates and emphasized its low stance. Finished in black, with its brushed silver roofline, looking as though it had just been driven off a Motorama stand, the Brougham was a tuxedo on wheels.

In his *Illustrated Cadillac Buyer's Guide*, Richard W. Langworth noted that "the Brougham was flashy where the [Lincoln] Mark II was understated, exotic where the Mark II was conventional." Many Cadillac Eldorado owners of that era wanted a showy, glitzy statement that proclaimed their *nouveau riche* status. Lincoln owners, who had paid $10,000 for the privilege of owning a Mark II, tended to be more of the conservative, old-money type.

Weighing in at 5,315 pounds, the Eldorado Brougham incorporated every power accessory Cadillac offered as standard, including a "memory" seat, cruise control, electrically operated doors, a power decklid opener, air conditioning, a dual-zone heating system, an automatic starter with a restart function, and low-profile tires with narrow-band whitewalls. The Brougham's ultra-luxurious glove compartment was accessorized with magnetized silver drink tumblers, cigarette and tissue dispensers, a holder for lipstick, a powder puff, an Arpège cologne atomizer with Lanvin perfume, and even a mirror and a matching leather notebook. Brougham buyers could choose from among forty-four combinations of interior and trim, includ-

ing Mouton lamb, Karakul (a black-furred Asian sheep), or soft lambskin carpeting.

Under the hood was a 365 cid, 325 bhp overhead valve V-8 with a 10:1 compression ratio, dual four-barrel carburetors, and dual exhausts. The Brougham's new air suspension system—a GM first, developed to counter the 1956 Packard "Torsion Level" suspension—employed four rubber air chambers, one at each wheel, that replaced conventional coil springs. Three load-levelers helped maintain a constant body height despite variation in road surface or passenger load. The new air suspension proved to be unreliable, and Cadillac dealers were forced to retrofit rear coil springs as a replacement.

Cadillac hoped to sell a thousand Eldorado Broughams in 1957, but the high price and the problems with its suspension held sales to four hundred. On the positive side, the Brougham inspired Cadillac and other automakers to produce limited-edition models and ensured that the Eldorado nameplate would be synonymous with engineering advances and distinctive styling. This car is lent by Gene and Marlene Epstein of Newtown, Pennsylvania.

1957
Jaguar XK-SS Roadster

Sir William Lyons, Jaguar's founding chairman, understood that great styling sold cars and that success in international racing sold still more of them. Although Jaguar production cars could be made very competitive, Lyons encouraged development of limited-production, faster, purpose-built racers. The first of these, known as the XK-C—or, more popularly, the C-Type—won the grueling 24 Hours of Le Mans in 1951, but failed to finish the race in 1952. Fitted in 1953 with then-radical Dunlop disc brakes, a team of factory C-Types swept Le Mans, finishing first, second, and fourth and confounding more expensive rivals like Mercedes-Benz and Ferrari, who had yet to develop the new type of brakes and competed with less-effective hydraulic drum brakes. The disc brakes permitted later braking before corners and remained virtually fade-proof over even the longest races.

In 1954 Jaguar produced a substantially improved version of this car with a stunning sheet-aluminum body and a stressed monocoque (one-piece) shell. Known as the D-Type, its detachable front sub-frame held a 250 bhp, 3.4-liter twin-cam inline-6 that was capable of more power with fine tuning. The newly revised engine featured a dry sump—the oil reservoir was a separate tank instead of a pan under the engine block. The resulting engine silhouette meant the entire car could be 30 percent lower than the C-Type and much more aerodynamic than its predecessor. Thanks to the work of Jaguar's chief stylist, the brilliant aerodynamicist Malcolm Sayer, the lithe D-Type was capable of topping 170 mph on the Mulsanne Straight at Le Mans. Competing in their first year at the famed twenty-four-hour event on the Sarthe Circuit, two factory D-Types retired, but the third factory entrant finished second behind the winning Ferrari 375 Plus, a racer with a much larger (4.5-liter) engine.

Undaunted, Jaguar revised the D-Type's bodywork and added a longer nose and a tall tail fin to further improve high-speed aerodynamics. The result was an unprecedented series of Le Mans wins in 1955 and 1956, and a remarkable finish in 1957 with D-Types taking the first four places. Geared appropriately, a D-Type could top 190 mph, making it the fastest sports car of its era. Except for the factory entries, all eighty-seven D-Types were short-nosed models. The D-Type became obsolete for FIA competition because of international rules that limited engine displacement to 3.0 liters.

That circumstance, along with a request from a special client, presented Lyons with an opportunity. Briggs S. Cunningham, a wealthy American sportsman who had earlier tried to win Le Mans with a team of his own Cunningham racing cars, wanted to compete with D-Types in the Sports Car Club of America (SCCA) competition. Available for sale in January of 1957, the XK-SS, essentially a road-going D-Type, was conceived as a "street car" to dominate production-class racing; SCCA rules required that at least fifty examples had to be built for the model to qualify—Jaguar already had thirty body shells and was ready to begin production.

The notion of a thinly disguised, barely de-tuned racer fitted with slightly more comfortable appointments for street use was a practice that Bugatti had pioneered in the 1920s with its road-going Grand Prix cars. In the postwar era, Ferrari and Aston Martin offered such cars, and Jaguar, which competed in a lower-priced bracket with its production models but often took the measure of its more expensive rivals on the track, wanted to do likewise. As a proven winner, the sleek, fast, and raucous D-Type represented the perfect platform.

Sayer designed a taller, plexiglass windshield for the XK-SS that curved around the front of the cockpit and was mated to detachable side windows (instead of flimsy canvas curtains). The cockpit was enlarged, padded, carpeted, and trimmed to a level befitting a top-of-the-line sports car. A snug-fitting canvas top was created, along with vestigial bumpers, small doors, and—as the fuel tank took up most of the rear—a luggage rack mounted on the tail panel. The completed car was spartan, but no more so than a Porsche Speedster, which had a tiny trunk and few creature comforts.

Available for sale in the United States at $7,500, the functionally beautiful XK-SS was nearly $3,000 less than a new Mercedes-Benz 300SLR roadster (see page 98), and, while not as luxurious, Jaguar's unabashed racer-for-the-road was significantly faster than its German rival. The company had intended to build more of this model if demand warranted, but a disastrous fire at the factory in Coventry destroyed the section where the XK-SS was produced. As a result, only sixteen examples were built and two additional cars were assembled from leftover parts for a total of eighteen.

Steve McQueen in his Jaguar XK-SS Roadster.

This example was owned by the Hollywood film star Steve McQueen. A high-performance car and motorcycle enthusiast—and a talented racer—McQueen took delight in terrorizing sections of Mulholland Drive, a twisty two-lane backroad that wound through the hills above Los Angeles. The Jaguar was later purchased and beautifully restored by Richard Freshman, who remembered seeing McQueen driving the car and vowed to someday own it. Freshman sold it to Robert E. Petersen, founder of the Petersen Automotive Museum, who liked purchasing cars with Hollywood celebrity history.

The D-Type Jaguar evolved in the late 1950s into the production E-Type, arguably the most elegant and affordable sports roadster of its era. Looking closely at the XK-SS's curvaceous flanks, tight cockpit, pinched waist, and low roofline, one can clearly see an E-Type in conception. This car is lent by Margie Petersen and the Petersen Automotive Museum, Los Angeles, California.

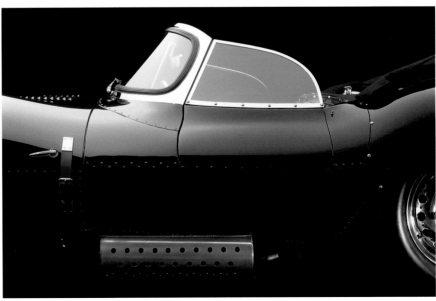

1959
Chevrolet Corvette Sting Ray

The Corvette Sting Ray prototype was developed through a fortunate confluence of automotive design and engineering talent, at a time when General Motors publicly wanted nothing to do with racing cars and competition. The protagonists included the irrepressible Bill Mitchell, Harley Earl's brilliant protégé and head of GM Styling; three talented designers: Pete Brock, Larry Shinoda, and Tony Lapine; the Corvette's legendary chief engineer, Zora Arkus-Duntov; and Dr. Dick Thompson, a racing dentist from Washington, D.C.

In the midst of an impressive General Motors career that began in 1935, William L. Mitchell succeeded Harley J. Earl in 1958 as the vice president of GM design. Writing in *Special-Interest Autos*, Robert C. Ackerson noted that GM's designs for 1959 "were even more garish and excessive than the '58s, but since the gap from styling prototype to production model is a span of a thousand days, there was little Mitchell could do to immediately demonstrate the change in command. In the case of the Corvette, however, there was an interesting option: the creation of a one-off special that would mark the beginning of Mitchell's reign."

Like all the North American automakers, General Motors had been a signatory to the 1957 Automobile Manufacturers Association industry-wide ban on racing. The 1957 Corvette SS racecar had been GM's first factory-initiated effort, but Chevrolet's limited-production sports car made just one competitive appearance, at Sebring, before the ban stopped its development. The fiery Mitchell would have no part of this. He and his staff had developed a razor-edge new Corvette design in 1957, but a recession and budget-cutting shelved the effort, seemingly for good.

Undaunted, Mitchell established "Studio X," a clandestine design center in the basement of the GM Styling administration building. Pete Brock, who later designed the Shelby Cobra Daytona Coupe, won an informal competition, sketching a sharp-edged coupe proposal that Mitchell later decided would be a roadster instead. Chuck Pohlman converted Brock's design into a roadster, and then Mitchell assigned the work to another studio, where it was massaged by Shinoda, Lapine, and Gene Garfinkle. Brock later told *Road & Track*'s John Lamm, "Mitchell came in and did the refinements. They refined the shape and made it even better."

Next, the project was moved to what was called "the hammer room," a fake tool locker behind which Mitchell had established a secret design studio so that work on the racecar could continue without senior executives knowing about the project. Mounted on the Corvette SS "mule" (development car) chassis, Mitchell's new Sting Ray prototype was finished to GM show-car standards with a smooth, shiny, and unfortunately rather heavy fiberglass body. To save time, the earlier Corvette SS had used a modified Mercedes-Benz 300 SL chassis. The Sting Ray had its own space-frame design with unequal-length A-arms in front and a De Dion independent rear end with trailing arms. Its engine was a 283 cid, 280 bhp fuel-injected Chevrolet V-8, and it was linked to a four-speed manual gearbox. The brakes, which would prove to be a weak point, were finned hydraulic drums, mounted conventionally in front and inboard at the rear.

The Sting Ray's good looks were enthusiastically received. In *Driving Style, GM's First Century*, Mark Cantey wrote: "His Corvette racer introduced the taut, razor-edged styling that would become the trademark of Mitchell's tailored designs in the 1960s. 'Trousers don't look any damn good without a crease in them. You've got to have an edge to accentuate form,' he [Mitchell] explained."

Bill Mitchell and his Sting Ray.

Incredibly, the Sting Ray effort was strictly a Bill Mitchell show. There was no GM nameplate on the car at first, since Chevrolet was officially out of racing. It was simply called the Mitchell Sting Ray. Mitchell had paid GM one dollar for the mule's remains, and he paid for the racing effort for two seasons out of his own pocket. The Sting Ray was fast, having turned a 183 mph lap at GM's Phoenix proving ground, although its aerodynamics were not ideal and the brakes were a disaster for racing. Its drum brakes were arguably the best of that era—Chrysler Center-Plane units, which had Al-Fin drums (aluminum cooling fins bonded to cast-iron drums)—but the Sting Ray's speed and heavy weight caused them to fade quickly under hard use.

On a tight track, during the car's first race at Marlboro, Maryland, driver Dick Thompson was leading Roger Penske, Augie Pabst, and Walt Hansgen (three of the era's top racecar drivers) before the brakes faded and he finished fourth. John Fitch had a similar experience at Elkhart Lake. GM's chief engineer Ed Cole had not accepted the efficacy of disc brakes—although Jaguar, Aston Martin, and Lotus were proving they could be very effective. Since disc brakes were not yet available on GM production models, the Sting Ray had to do without. Even so, the uncanny driving ability of Thompson, "the flying dentist," made the overweight Sting Ray competitive.

After the Sting Ray received a lighter body for 1960, Thompson won the 1960 Sports Car Club of America (SCCA) "C Modified" Championship against the formidable Reventlow Scarabs. Zora Arkus-Duntov, father of the high-performance Corvette, who had spearheaded the Corvette SS project, was reportedly miffed that the Sting Ray was perceived as an official GM project, though he had not worked on it and there was no real factory support. After the 1960 Series, because it was his personal car, Mitchell had the Sting Ray re-bodied again, this time with a passenger-side windscreen and Corvette badges, and out it went on the show circuit, at first repainted red and finally silver again, as it is today.

Few spectators who saw the Sting Ray in competition would have predicted that the car's futuristic styling would be adopted for the production 1963 Corvette Sting Ray split-window coupe and subsequently for the roadster version. Looking at the Sting Ray prototype today—with its prominent driver-side fairing, racy low windscreens, Halibrand "kidney bean" knockoff wheels, and sweeping side pipes—the bodywork still appears contemporary. Mitchell and his colleagues were ahead of their time, and it shows. The car is lent by the General Motors Heritage Center, Warren, Michigan.

1961
Aston Martin DB4GT Zagato

NO. 0187/L

The British sports car specialist Aston Martin was founded in 1914. Carrozzeria Zagato, one of Italy's finest coachbuilders, began just five years later. Countries and cultures apart, the two firms did not work together until 1960. By then, Aston Martin had competed successfully in racing and, under the stewardship of John Wyer, developed the remarkable DBR (which won the 24 Hours of Le Mans in 1959) and the short-wheelbase DB4GT, a limited-production Gran Turismo that raced competitively against Ferrari and Maserati. Prior to World War II, Ugo Zagato's flowing designs for Vittorio Jano's spirited Alfa Romeo sports and racing cars established that marque as a winner for all time.

From the mid-1940s to the late 1950s, Elio Zagato, Ugo's oldest son, developed his own distinctive aerodynamic design language before he was injured in a road accident. Elio's brother Gianni Zagato then joined the venerable Milanese company and invited Ercole Spada, a talented twenty-three-year-old designer, to work with him. Wyer and Zagato met at the London Earl's Court Motor Show in 1959 and formed a partnership in which Carrozzeria Zagato would build custom bodies for a small series of competition DB4GTs. The first Aston lightweight chassis arrived in Italy early the following year. The cars that emerged would become legends.

Spada's design for the DB4GT resembled Ferrari's successful 250 GT Short-wheelbase Berlinetta (SWB) (see page 128), but many critics insist the sensuous Zagato/Spada shape is bolder, more aggressive, and arguably more contemporary. From the sneer of its fierce, turned-down, oversized grille to the trio of distinctive hood bulges, delicately flared fenders, twin outside filler caps nestled in the fenderwells, low, tight cabin, and rounded (almost impudent) tail with its siamesed pair of bellowing tailpipes, the DB4GT Zagato exudes a purposefulness matched by its fine record as a quick, agile, and race-winning GT. Under license from Carrozzeria Touring, also of Milan, these lovely Zagato bodies used the *Superleggera* (super-light) construction technique, a thin skin of aluminum stretched over a network of small-diameter steel tubing.

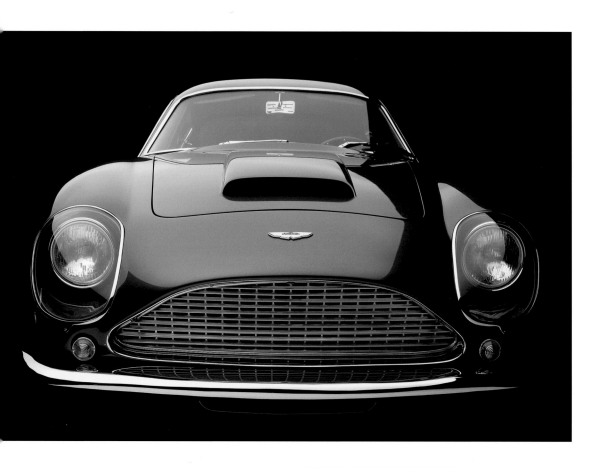

Aston Martin DB4GT Zagato coupe in the 1972 Wiscombe Hill Climb.

High-performance Aston DB4s had more than just a pretty dress to wear. Under the hood was a hyper-tuned version of the 3.7-liter twin-cam six designed by Tadek Marek, fitted with twin distributors, two sets of spark plugs, a 9.7:1 high-compression cylinder head, hotter camshafts, and triple Weber carburetors. The output was a torrid 314 bhp, enabling the cars to go from 0-to-60 in six seconds and to race head-to-head with the SWB's successor, the Ferrari 250 GTO. Ninety-five lightweight Aston DB4GT coupes were built—seventy-five with factory bodies, just nineteen hand-formed aluminum Zagato coupes, and a lone example created by Carrozzeria Bertone. Raced by such driving luminaries as Jimmy Clark, Roy Salvadori, Stirling Moss, and Innes Ireland, the Zagato-bodied DB4GTs were as fast as the lighter Ferrari GTOs but not as consistent.

This example, 0187/L, was the Turin show car in 1961, "dressed up" with bumpers, a chrome strip along the side, chrome instead of polished aluminum around the windows and headlights, and chrome wheels. It is believed that only two of these cars had hood scoops, and this is one of them. Of the nineteen examples built, just six were left-hand drive. David Sydorick, who owns 0187/L, is a Zagato coachwork enthusiast who had searched for a Zagato Aston for years. After considerable research, he located Nicholas Begovich, a California Institute of Technology Ph.D. who, in Sydorick's words, "had many cars in his garages, like a Porsche Speedster and a Porsche 904 racer, and didn't talk to anybody. He'd buy a car at the factory, drive it around a little, then bring it home and take it apart." Begovich had purchased the Aston from an Italian owner in 1968, and the car had not run in years. The first time Sydorick visited Begovich, he saw the Aston Zagato under a cover.

Realizing that inquiries about the Zagato might not be appreciated, David and his wife Ginny became friends with Nick and Lee Begovich, and Sydorick gradually earned Begovich's affection and respect. Ultimately, Sydorick learned that Begovich wanted to donate the car to Cal Tech, and that he would eventually have to purchase the car from the University, which he was finally able to do. Begovich had removed the rear axle in 1971, and had worked on the gas tank, but the rest of the prized Aston lightweight was all together. It had sat in one spot for thirty years.

Sydorick involved Begovich in the selection of a restorer and in the restoration process. After considerable deliberation, he arranged for the car to be restored by Steel Wings, an Aston specialist now located in Hopewell, New Jersey. Prior to the restoration, Sydorick agonized over whether to have the car's hood restored with the factory scoop or the three blisters; he was not pleased with either treatment, but he did not want to change the car. In the end, after receiving advice from noted collector Miles Collier (who said, "Let the car tell you"), Sydorick had a second hood made, without the "bumps and the scoops," and he had the bumpers designed so they could easily be removed. Since the completion of the restoration in 2002, 0187/L has won its class convincingly every time it has been shown. In 2003 it won Best of Show at the

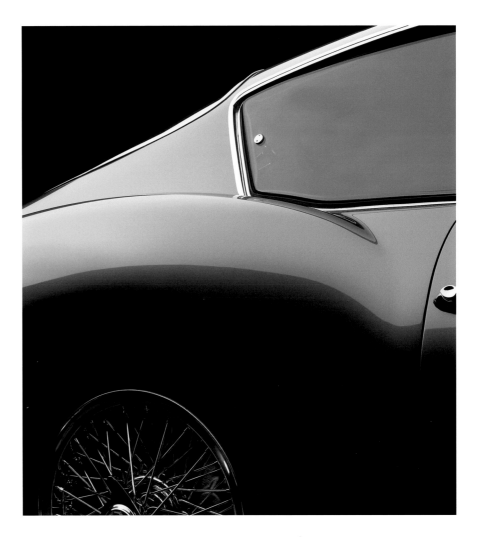

Aston Martin National Meet in Lime Rock, Connecticut, and it won its class at the Pebble Beach Concours d'Elegance the same year. It took the prestigious Road & Track award at the 2004 Amelia Island Concours, won awards at the Villa d'Este event on Lake Como, and was named Best of Show at the 2005 Goodwood Festival of Speed. The car is lent by David and Ginny Sydorick of Beverly Hills, California.

1961
Ferrari 250 GT Comp./61 Short-wheelbase Berlinetta

S/N 2689

In 1947 Battista "Pinin" Farina (who changed his name and that of his company to Pininfarina in 1958) created the first modern Italian sports coupe body for Cisitalia. On that landmark Berlinetta (Italian for "sports coupe"), the hood line was noticeably lower than the car's fenders, and the sleek horizontal grille and unadorned slab sides were considered a very modern approach. Many Italian *carrozzerie*—including Ghia, Allemano, Vignale, Zagato, and Bertone—vied for commissions to design and build Ferrari production car bodies, but by the late 1950s the Milanese firm of Industrie Pininfarina S.p.A. had become the predominant supplier.

In 1958 Enzo Ferrari wanted to improve the road-racing performance of his already very successful 250 GT (Gran Turismo) long-wheelbase Berlinetta, popularly known as the Tour de France, after its considerable success in that intense road-racing series. Although the 250 GT long-wheelbase Berlinetta was visually stunning, Ferrari and his engineers elected to shorten the wheelbase (the distance between wheel centers) from 102⁵⁄₁₆ inches to 95³⁄₁₆ inches, reinforce the frame, and improve the suspension with tubular shock absorbers and a stouter ⅝-inch front anti-roll bar.

Battista Pininfarina and his talented staff refined and updated the coachwork, and Carrozzeria Scaglietti in Modena began hand-building the bodies in aluminum alloy and steel. Arguably the last true dual-purpose Ferrari—road-going and -racing—the 250 GT short-wheelbase Berlinetta was considered smartly contemporary in its day, without losing any of its distinctive visual characteristics.

Abbreviating the wheelbase by seven inches enhanced the Ferrari's cornering and maneuverability. The output of its 3.0-liter, single-overhead-camshaft V-12 was increased from 250 bhp to as much as 285 bhp with large Weber twin-choke carburetors in conjunction with improvements to the camshafts and the valve timing. The "250" refers to the cubic capacity (250 cc), which, when multiplied by the number of cylinders, is 3,000 cc or 3.0-liters. The transmission was a four-speed, close-ratio manual gearbox (steel for street cars, finned alloy for competition models) mounted conventionally behind the engine. Independant double wishbones in front and a solid rear axle with leaf springs and

S/N 2689 won its class at Le Mans in 1961.

radius rods constituted the suspension arrangement. A rigid frame, fashioned from oval-shaped tubing, ensured that the 250 GT had the stiffness required of a genuine road/racing sports coupe. Two versions were offered; the competition cars had light alloy bodywork, which often included an outside-mounted flip-up fuel filler and a raised hood scoop with a cold-air box for the three Weber carburetors. The brakes were Dunlop hydraulic discs.

Pininfarina's coachwork design was elegantly drawn, with a rectangular, "egg-crate" Ferrari grille, snugly fitting fenders that resembled a tight shirt stretched over a muscular torso, a sharply raked windscreen, a snug cabin, and a low roofline that tapered gracefully rearward. The 250 SWB's beautiful yet purposeful shape came to define the long-hood short-deck style that was soon imitated by many rivals, including Ford's later Mustang fastback. Alloy-bodied, stripped-for-action competition 250 SWBs weighed about 200 pounds less than the steel-bodied versions. The latter versions, known as *Lusso* (luxury) models, had stylish leather interiors, comfortable padded bucket seats, additional soundproofing, and were usually supplied in a milder state of tune than the racing versions.

The Ferrari factory and its customers lost no time in racing the new 250 SWB. The first models competed at Le Mans in 1959 in the GT class. Borrani center-locking wire wheels were standard equipment, and some competition cars had subtly flared rear fenders to accommodate larger tires. Lightweight bumpers in both the front and rear did little for body protection, and where the rules permitted, many cars were run without them. Just 165 250 GT short-wheelbase Berlinettas were built from 1959 to 1962: 90 steel cars and 75 alloy-bodied versions.

To compete in the World Constructor's Championship, Ferrari built a series of eighteen special 250 SWBs in 1961. A lightweight chassis and an even lighter alloy body combined to save precious weight, and the V-12 was modified to produce 285 bhp. Officially called Comp./61s and popularly known as "SEFAC hot rods" (Società Esercizio Fabbriche Automobili e Corse), modified SWBs could be geared to top 160 mph on long stretches, such as the Mulsanne Straight on the Sarthe Circuit of the 24 Hours of Le Mans.

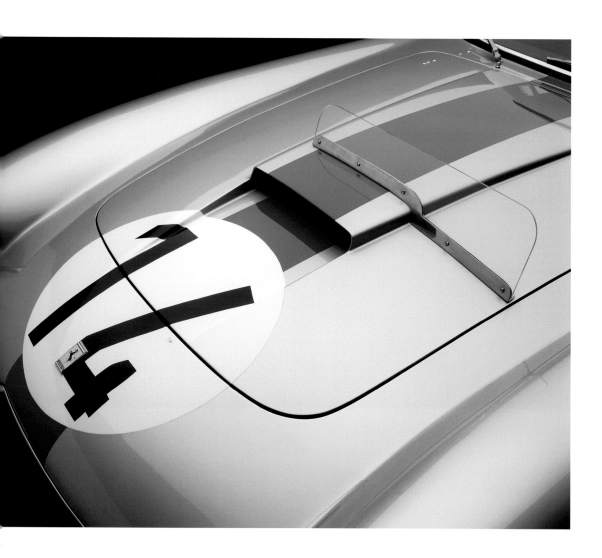

This example, S/N 2689—an ultra-lightweight Berlinetta with a bare interior, an outside fuel filler cap, a hood-mounted bug screen, and a pit light on its rear fender—was one of the most successful SWB competition cars. It won the GT Class and finished third overall at the 24 Hours of Le Mans in 1961, driven by Pierre Noblet and Jean Guichet. Next, it won the Coppa Inter Europa at Monza, again driven by Noblet. At the Monterey Coupes du Salon, driven by Guichet, the S/N 2689 was sidelined by engine failure. After a complete rebuild at the Ferrari factory, the car competed well at Spa and Auvergne; Noblet then won the 1962 Coupe de Bruxelles and turned the fastest lap. S/N 2689 finished second overall at the 500-kilometer race of Spa and second in class at the 1,000 kilometers of the Nürburgring. During the 1962 Le Mans trials, driven by Willy Mairesse, S/N 2689 was clocked at 164.6 mph on the Mulsanne Straight and its best average lap was 115.6 mph. SEFAC hot rods like this one were the most advanced Ferrari competition Berlinettas before the advent of the legendary Ferrari 250 GTO, and they remain the most desirable 250 SWB Ferraris.

Its active competition life over, S/N 2689 was sold to a buyer in Rome in 1965. It then went to the United States to a series of owners that included Ferrari aficionado Ed Niles, well-known exotic car dealer Harley Cluxton, and J. R. Upton. A total restoration began in 1975 and was completed in 1984, with the car appearing once again in its 1961 Le Mans GT Class-winning livery. In 2003 this storied Berlinetta received a cosmetic restoration by Ferrari specialist Wayne Obry. The present owner enjoys driving the car; the fierce crackle of its four-pipe exhaust is sufficient to bring a smile to any enthusiast's face. The car is lent by Bruce and Raylene Meyer of Beverly Hills, California.

Glossary of Technical Terms

Brake horsepower (abbreviated **bhp**) is the measure of an engine's horsepower without the loss in power caused by the gearbox, generator, differential, water pump, and other auxiliary components.

Cubic-inch displacement (abbreviated **cid**) is the volume swept by all the pistons in an internal combustion engine. Power is directly proportional to cid.

Desmodromic valves are positively closed by a cam-and-leverage system, rather than relying on the more conventional valve springs, which were a limitation on high-revving engine performance because of metal fatigue.

Dry sump lubrication, as opposed to the conventional oil-pan reservoir, uses a separate tank for the engine oil, in order to function well under racing conditions.

Flathead engines were used by most cars prior to the 1950s because they were less expensive to manufacture. In a flathead engine, the valves are in the block, rather than in the head, and they open in a chamber beside the piston.

In a **Hemi engine**, the top of the combustion chamber is shaped like half of a sphere and the engine is said to have "hemispherical heads." In a Hemi head, the spark plug is normally located at the top of the combustion chamber, and the valves open on opposite sides of the combustion chamber.

Overhead camshaft is the type of valve train arrangement in which an engine's camshaft is in its cylinder head. When the camshaft is close to the valves, the valve train's parts can be stiffer and lighter, allowing the valves to open and close quickly. In a single overhead cam, one camshaft actuates all of the valves. In a double overhead cam, one camshaft actuates the intake valve and the other operates the exhaust valves.

A **supercharger** is an air compressor that provides extra oxygen under pressure for an internal combustion engine, allowing more fuel to be used per cycle, increasing the power output of the engine.

Superleggera is an automobile construction technology used in Italy from the middle of the twentieth century. The name means "super light" in Italian, and was coined in 1937 by the Italian coachbuilder Carrozzeria Touring. Unlike the monocoque and body-on-frame methods widely adopted by the 1950s, *Superleggera* cars use a full-body frame of metal tubes that closely follows the shape of the car. These are then covered with body panels, made of aluminium. The *Superleggera* frame tubes are too small and of unsuitable material for mounting suspension components. This distinguishes it very clearly from spaceframe construction, where no separate chassis is required.

Wheelbase measurement is the horizontal distance between the center of the front wheel and the center of the rear wheel.

Further Reading

Adatto, Richard. *From Passion to Perfection: The Story of French Streamlined Styling*. Paris: Editions SPE Barthelemy, 2002.

Adatto, Richard S., and Diana E. Meredith. *Delage: Styling and Design*. Deerfield, Illinois: Dalton Watson Fine Books, 2005.

———. *Delahaye: Styling and Design*. Philadelphia: Coachbuilt Press, 2006.

Adler, Dennis. *The Art of the Automobile: The 100 Greatest Cars*. New York: HarperCollins, 2000.

———. *Duesenberg*. Iola, Wisconsin: Krause Publications, 2004.

Antonick, Michael. *Illustrated Corvette Buyer's Guide*. Osceola, Wisconsin: Motorbooks International, 1990.

Barrett, Frank. *Illustrated Mercedes-Benz Buyer's Guide*. Osceola, Wisconsin: Motorbooks International, 1998.

Bill, Jon M. *Duesenberg Racecars and Passenger Cars Photo Archive*. Hudson, Wisconsin: Iconografix, 2005.

Brazendale, Kevin. *Great Cars of the Golden Age*. New York: Crescent Books, 1976.

Butler, Don. *Auburn Cord Duesenberg*. Osceola, Wisconsin: Motorbooks International, 1992.

Cantey, Mark R. *Driving Style: GM Design's First Century*. Charlotte, North Carolina: MRC Publishing, 2008.

Carlson, Richard Burns. *The Olympian Cars*. Brattleboro, Vermont: Beaver's Pond Press, 1998.

Clark, Henry Austin Jr., Ralph Dunwoodie, Beverly Rae Kimes, and Keith Marvin. *Standard Catalog of American Cars, 1805–1942*. 2nd ed. Iola, Wisconsin: Krause Publications, 1989.

Cotter, Tom. *The Cobra in the Barn: Great Stories of Automotive Archaeology*. Osceola, Wisconsin: Motorbooks International, 2005.

Cumberford, Robert, and Michael Zumbrunn. *Auto Legends: Classics of Style and Design*. London: Merrell, 2004.

Decrey, Lionel, Jean-Louis Fatio, and Pierre-Yves Laugier. *Bugatti, Les 57 Sport*. Volume II. Corseaux, Switzerland: Editions Bugattibook, 2004.

Eastman, Art. "Porsche's First Pure Race Car: 550-01." *Vintage Motorsport* (September/October 2006).

Fenster, J. M. *Packard: The Pride*. Kutztown, Pennsylvania: Automobile Quarterly Publications, 1989.

Fetherston, David, and Tony Thacker. *Chrysler Concept Cars, 1940–1970*. North Branch, Minnesota: CarTech, 2007.

Georgano, Nick, ed. *The Beaulieu Encyclopedia of the Automobile*. Volumes I–III. London: The Stationery Office, 2001.

———. *The Beaulieu Encyclopedia of the Automobile: Coachbuilding*. London: The Stationery Office, 2001.

Gist, Peter. *Virgil Exner: Visioneer*. Dorchester, England: Velcoe Publishing, 2007.

Gross, Ken. *Ferrari 250GT SWB: The Definitive Road-Race Car*. London: Osprey Publishing/Motorbooks International, 1985.

Gunnell, John. *Standard Guide to 1950s American Cars*. Iola, Wisconsin: Krause Publications, 2004.

Holls, Dave, and Michael Lamm. *A Century of Automotive Style: 100 Years of American Car Design*. Stockton, California: Lamm-Morada Publishing, 1996.

Horsley, Fred. *Dream Cars*. Los Angeles: Trend, Inc., 1953.

Jenkinson, Denis. *Porsche 356*. London: Osprey Publishing, 1980.

Kimes, Beverly Rae. *The Classic Era*. Des Plaines, Illinois: Classic Car Club of America, 2001.

———. *Packard: A History of the Motorcar and the Company*. Princeton, Indiana: Princeton Publishing, Inc., 1978.

Lamm, John. "Chevrolet Corvette Sting Ray." *Road & Track* (July 2001).

Langworth, Richard M. *Illustrated Cadillac Buyer's Guide*. Osceola, Wisconsin: Motorbooks International, 1986.

———. *Illustrated Packard Buyer's Guide*. Osceola, Wisconsin: Motorbooks International, 1998.

Lentinello, Richard. *The Hemmings Motor News Book of Corvettes*. Bennington, Vermont: Watering, Inc., 2000.

Ludvigsen, Karl. *Porsche: Excellence Was Expected*. Volumes I–III. Cambridge, Massachusetts: Bentley Publishers, 2003.

Ludvigsen, Karl, ed. *Porsche Spyders*. Hudson, Wisconsin: Iconografix, 2002.

Maley, George. "The Von Krieger 540K Special Roadster." *The Star* (May/June 1999).

Malks, Josh B. *Illustrated Duesenberg Buyer's Guide*. Osceola, Wisconsin: Motorbooks International, 1993.

Melin, Jan. *Mercedes-Benz: The Supercharged 8-Cylinder Cars of the 1930s*. Gothenburg, Sweden: Nordbook International Co-Editions, 1985.

Moore, Simon. *The Immortal 2.9*. Seattle: Parkside Publications, 2008.

Murray, Spence, ed. *Corvette: An American Classic*. Los Angeles: Petersen Publishing Co., 1978.

Pearson, Charles T. *The Indomitable Tin Goose: The True Story of Preston Tucker and His Car*. Minneapolis: Motorbooks International, 1974.

Pfau, Hugo. *The Coachbuilt Packard*. London: Dalton Watson Publishers, 1973.

Pourret, Jess G. *Ferrari 250GT Competition Cars*. Somerset, England: Haynes Publishing Group, 1977.

Purdy, Ken W. *The Porsche Story*. Stuttgart: Porsche, AG, 1964.

Sparke, Penny. *A Century of Car Design*. Hauppauge, New York: Barron's Educational Series, 2002.

Speed, Style, and Beauty: Cars from the Ralph Lauren Collection. Edited by Beverly Rae Kimes and Winston Goodfellow. Boston: Museum of Fine Arts, Boston, 2005.

Stein, Jonathan, ed. *The Art and Colour of General Motors*. Philadelphia: Coachbuilt Press, 2008.

———. *Curves of Steel: Streamlined Automobile Design at the Phoenix Art Museum*. Philadelphia: Coachbuilt Press, 2007.

Stone, Matt. *McQueen's Machines: The Cars and Bikes of a Hollywood Icon*. Saint Paul: Motorbooks International, 2007.

Takashima, Shizuo. "Andre Dubonnet's Ravishing Hisso." *Special-Interest Autos* (January–February 1978).

Vintage Motor Cars in Arizona, 2005. RM Auctions Catalogs. Blenheim, Ontario: RM Auctions, Inc., 2005.

Vintage Motor Cars in Arizona, 2006. RM Auctions Catalogs. Blenheim, Ontario: RM Auctions, Inc., 2006.

Vintage Motor Cars in Arizona, 2009. RM Auctions Catalogs. Blenheim, Ontario: RM Auctions, Inc., 2009.

Willson, Quentin. *The Ultimate Classic Car Book*. London: Dorling Kindersley Limited, 1995.

Woodenberg, Paul R. *Illustrated Aston Martin Buyer's Guide*. Osceola, Wisconsin: Motorbooks International, 1986.

Zeyer, Jurgen. "At First Glance." *Christophorus* 336 (February/March 2009).

Lenders to the Exhibition

1930 Bentley Speed Six "Blue Train Special" (Portland only)
Bruce and Jolene McCaw, Seattle, Washington

1931 Duesenberg SJ Convertible Sedan (Portland only)
Tom and Susan Armstrong, Issaquah, Washington

1933 Pierce-Arrow Silver Arrow
Don Williams and the Blackhawk Collection of Danville, California

1934 Packard LeBaron Runabout Speedster (Atlanta only)
Robert and Sandra Bahre of Alton, New Hampshire

1935 Duesenberg JN Roadster (Atlanta only)
Sam and Emily Mann of Englewood Cliffs, New Jersey

1937 Bugatti Type 57S Atalante
William E. (Chip) Connor, II, of Deepwater Bay, Hong Kong

1937 Delage D8-120S (Atlanta only)
Sam and Emily Mann of Englewood Cliffs, New Jersey

1937 Dubonnet Hispano-Suiza H-6C "Xenia"
Merle and Peter Mullin and the Peter Mullin Automotive Museum
Foundation, Beverly Hills, California

1937 Mercedes-Benz 540K Special Roadster
Lee and Joan Herrington of Bow, New Hampshire

1938 Alfa Romeo 8C2900B Touring Berlinetta
Jon and Mary Shirley of Bellevue, Washington

1938–1939 Porsche Type 64 Body Shell (Atlanta only)
The Porsche Museum

1939 Talbot-Lago T-150-C-SS (Portland only)
Deborah and Arturo Keller of the Pyramid Collection, Petaluma, California

1948 Tucker Model 48 Torpedo No. 1007 (Portland only)
The LeMay Family Collection, compliments of America's Car Museum,
Tacoma, Washington

1948 Tucker Model 48 Torpedo (Atlanta only)
The Marital Trust ULWT of Gene S. Cofer and the Cofer Collection, Tucker,
Georgia

1953 Porsche 550
Miles Collier and The Collier Collection, Naples, Florida

1954 Dodge Firearrow III
David J. Disiere of Irving, Texas

1955 Mercedes-Benz 300SLR "Uhlenhaut" Coupe
Mercedes-Benz Museum, Stuttgart, Germany

1957 Cadillac Eldorado Brougham (Atlanta only)
Gene and Marlene Epstein of Newtown, Pennsylvania

1957 Jaguar XK-SS Roadster
Margie Petersen and the Petersen Automotive Museum,
Los Angeles, California

1959 Chevrolet Corvette Sting Ray
General Motors Heritage Center, Warren, Michigan

1961 Aston Martin DB4GT Zagato Coupe
David and Ginny Sydorick of Beverly Hills, California

1961 Ferrari 250 GT Comp./61 Short-wheelbase Berlinetta
Bruce and Raylene Meyer of Beverly Hills, California

Index

Photo Credits

The publisher gratefully acknowledges the following people and institutions for the photographs in this book.

Peter Harholdt: cover, pages 1, 2–3, 5, 8, 25–31, 32–37, 38–43, 44–48, 50–52, 54–60, 62–67 left, 75–81, 83–89, 91, 104 bottom–113, 114 right–121 left, 122–124 left and bottom, 125–127, 128 bottom–133

The Museum of Modern Art Archives, The Museum of Modern Art, New York: page 11

Michael Lamm, Lamm-Morada Publishing Co. Inc.: pages 12, 22, 82

Auburn Cord Duesenberg Automobile Museum, Auburn, Indiana: page 13

The Huntington Library, San Marino, California, "Dick" Whittington Collection: page 15

Chrysler Group LLC: pages 17, 97 left

High Museum of Art: page 18

Ron Kimball / www.kimballstock.com, courtesy Pebble Beach Concours d'Elegance: pages 19, 23

Porsche Werkfotos: pages 20, 78

Charlie Lyttle, courtesy Jon and Mary Shirley and the International Motor Racing Research Center at Watkins Glen: page 21

Auburn University Libraries: page 43

mptvimages.com: page 43

William E. (Chip) Connor II: page 49

Hemmings Motor News: page 53

Lee and Joan Herrington: page 61

Arthur Richards, Jr., courtesy Jon and Mary Shirley and International Motor Racing Research Center at Watkins Glen: page 73 right

Frank M. Orel, courtesy Porsche AG, Porsche Museum Stuttgart, and Porsche Cars North America: pages 68–71, 73

The Collier Collection: page 90

RM Auctions / Darin Schnabel: pages 92–96, 97 right

Mercedes-Benz Classic: pages 98–103

General Motors and Jean-Michel Roux: page 104 top

c 1978 Sid Avery / mptvimages.com: page 114 left

General Motors Portrait Files: page 121 right

Roger Stowers, courtesy Aston Martin Heritage Trust: page 124 right

Bruce Meyer: page 128 top